ELECTION DAY REGISTRATION

ELECTION DAY REGISTRATION

THE MINNESOTA AND WISCONSIN EXPERIENCE IN 1976

Richard G. Smolka

American Enterprise Institute for Public Policy Research
Washington, D.C.

Richard G. Smolka is professor of political science at American University and editor of *Election Administration Reports*.

ISBN 0-8447-3263-X

AEI Studies 164

Library of Congress Catalog Card No. 77-83209

Printed in the United States of America

CONTENTS

PREFACE

This study describes and analyzes election day registration at the polls. It is concerned primarily with the procedures that were used and results that were experienced in Minnesota and Wisconsin during the presidential election of November 1976.

President Jimmy Carter made election day registration at the polls the major element in his proposed Universal Voter Registration Act of 1977 and gave it a high priority in his election reform program for the year. President Carter is especially knowledgeable about election procedures. In his book, *Why Not the Best?* he devoted a considerable portion of one chapter, "First Politics," to his personal observations of election day procedures and to his efforts to curb fraudulent voting practices in Georgia.

Carter's approach marked a departure from a six-year Democratic effort, led by former Senator Gale W. McGee of Wyoming, to establish a national voter registration agency and a system of voter registration by mail. Although this effort failed in Congress, eighteen states and the District of Columbia adopted some form of general registration by mail between 1973 and 1976. During the 1976 presidential election, about 47 percent of the voting age population lived in states in which all voters were able to register by mail.

The increased turnout anticipated by the sponsors of mail registration failed to occur. Combined turnout in all states with mail registration declined about 2 percentage points, but the turnout showed no decline in states without mail registration. In the five states which permitted the voters to register on election day, however, the turnout increased. Two states, Minnesota and Wisconsin, instituted election day registration after the 1972 election, and each showed increases of more than 3 percentage points in 1976.

North Dakota, which has no voter registration requirement and no permanent registration, increased less than 1 percentage point from 1972. Maine and Oregon, which permitted voters to register in a central location on election day prior to going to the polls, also showed increases over 1972 turnout rates—4.1 percentage points in Maine and 0.6 percentage points in Oregon.

Because Minnesota and Wisconsin were the only states with election day registration at the polls as part of a statewide permanent voter registration system, they provide the most useful information about the operation of the system. Neither state is "typical" in voter registration history because both had long permitted persons who reside in smaller communities to vote without registering. Wisconsin retained this feature even with its new law.

This study analyzes the administrative details of voter registration, such as the voter registration form, the affidavits, and the procedures used to register voters and to detect or prevent vote fraud. The emphasis is on the conduct of election administrators and polling place officials, but the role of law enforcement officials is also described. A serious attempt was made to distinguish factors intrinsic to any system of election day voter registration from those resulting from administrative decisions made during a presidential election year, without prior experience from which to estimate the probable number of election day registrants.

Chapter 1 provides a general background of the purposes and practices of voter registration in the United States. Chapters 2 and 3 describe the election laws and voter registration systems of Minnesota and Wisconsin respectively, the administrative procedures used to register voters, and the results of voter registration at the polls. The fourth chapter assesses the impact of election day registration on preregistration, on voter turnout, and on administrative procedures, and identifies the potential of vote fraud made possible by the procedure. A summary concludes the study.

For several years, the election officials of Minnesota and Wisconsin have been most cooperative in providing the author with data, legal interpretations of election law, statistics, and election related materials. Once again, during this study, these officials—especially Joan Anderson Growe, secretary of state of Minnesota, Gerald J. Ferwerda, executive secretary, Wisconsin State Elections Board, Thaddeus C. Stawicki, executive secretary, City of Milwaukee Board of Election Commissioners, and Lyall A. Schwartzkopf, Minneapolis city clerk —were extremely helpful in providing assistance.

Many other officials were interviewed in person and offered primary source material, described elections procedures, and offered personal observations. From Minnesota, these include Mary Ann McCoy, Elections Division, Office of the Secretary of State; Rose Mix, city clerk and Walter Bell, director of elections, St. Paul; Arthur Jensen, city clerk, Bloomington; Lucille Aurelius, city clerk, Maplewood; Carole Grimm, city clerk, Rochester; John Streitz, city clerk, St. Cloud; Betty Bell, city clerk, Coon Rapids; and Helen Schendel, city clerk-treasurer, Milaca. From Wisconsin, they include Eldon Hoel, city clerk and Thomas J. Schwartz, deputy city clerk, Madison; Paul Janquart, city clerk, Green Bay; Lawrence Felten, city clerk, Sheboygan; James R.

Neuman, city clerk, Wauwatosa; Eldon Rinka, city clerk, West Allis; Eunice Niemi, executive secretary, Milwaukee County Board of Supervisors, and E. Michael McCann, district attorney, Milwaukee County.

In addition, telephone interviews were conducted with the county auditors of the ten largest Minnesota counties and with the district attorney of the ten largest Wisconsin counties or a responsible assistant from each jurisdiction. The assistance of each of these persons is gratefully acknowledged.

A note of thanks is also due to Austin Ranney and Jeane Kirkpatrick, two outstanding scholars of political parties and elections who read and commented on the draft manuscript; to Jerome J. Hanus, an American University colleague; and to Dennis and Rebecca Farrell who rendered timely assistance. Finally, and more personally the author owes a special debt of gratitude to his son Gregory for work on the calculator and to Mary Wason for prompt and accurate typing under deadline pressure.

1
HISTORY AND PURPOSE OF VOTER REGISTRATION LAWS

Voter registration in the United States establishes that the person who registers is a citizen, a resident, and a qualified voter from the address from which he offers to vote. When communities were smaller and populations more stable, there was little need for voter registration. Most people knew their neighbors, and residents were easily identified even if they were not known personally by election officials. As populations increased, particularly through immigration, it became necessary to determine voter eligibility in advance of the election to prevent voting by unqualified persons.

History

Fear of the voting tendencies of the new immigrants, as well as rather widespread fraud, led to the adoption of restrictive legislation on voter registration, including citizenship qualifications for voting and voter registration laws.

In his classic study of voter registration, Joseph P. Harris wrote that before the enactment of voter registration laws, "it was not unusual for armed men to appear at the polls and demand the right to vote. . . ."[1] According to Harris, these persons were permitted to vote and then were never seen again. Elections, he said, turned into riots and shooting matches.

The voter registration process has been subjected to several kinds of abuses over the years. Early registration requirements of the nineteenth century were sometimes related more to taxes than to voting and were used as a means of identifying taxpayers. Even in

---

[1]Joseph P. Harris, *Registration of Voters in the United States* (Washington, D.C.: The Brookings Institution, 1928), p. 6.

1977, fear of this practice prompted the U.S. Senate to amend the Overseas Citizens Voting Rights Act to ensure that no citizen who exercised his voting rights under the act would be subjected to federal, state, or local tax merely for doing so.

Registry lists were advocated by the Whigs in the early part of the nineteenth century both to prevent fraudulent repeat voting, which occurred with regularity, and to restrict voting by less desirable persons. Registry laws of the 1830s included a tax that effectively reduced voter turnout in Rhode Island, Philadelphia, and New York City.[2]

From the post Civil War period through the mid-twentieth century, the registration process was used in the South to restrict the rights of blacks to vote. Long and complicated voter registration forms, unreasonable identification requirements, inconvenient hours and places of registration, literacy tests, and other such devices were employed to deny blacks their voting rights. Ultimately, the Civil Rights acts of 1957 and subsequent years and the Voting Rights acts of 1965, 1970, and 1975 offered substantial protection to racial minorities. In northern cities, manipulation of the registration lists, selective purging of names of voters, and partisan treatment in the identification of registered voters at the polls was not uncommon.

Types of Voter Registration. The first modern systems of voter registration in the United States required voters to reregister every one, two, or four years, depending upon state law. Widely in use about the turn of the century, this periodic registration was superseded by "permanent" voter registration systems, in which the voter's name remained on the rolls unless he died, moved away, changed his name, or was disqualified from voting. The permanent lists required periodic "purging" to remove the names of persons no longer eligible to vote and to maintain current and accurate lists of registered voters. Purges were conducted by door-to-door canvasses, by mail canvasses, or simply by removing the names of persons who failed to vote within a prescribed period. Because many states purged lists for failure to vote within a two-year period, persons who participated only in presidential elections were little better off than they had been under the older form of periodic registration. Such persons were required to reregister even though they had previously registered and had not moved. By 1960, most of the states had adopted a form of permanent voter registration. Public attention became less preoccupied with vote fraud and more concerned with the effect voter registration procedure had on voter

---

[2] For details of early voter registration laws and effects, see Chilton Williamson, *American Suffrage From Property to Democracy 1760–1860* (Princeton: Princeton University Press, 1960).

turnout. Registration laws began to be regarded as major obstacles to voting.[3]

The President's Commission. In November 1963, the President's Commission on Registration and Voting Participation, created by President John F. Kennedy, reported that "restrictive legal and administrative procedures in registration and voting disenfranchise millions."[4] To promote greater participation the commission offered twenty-one specific recommendations. These included the following proposals: to extend voter registration as close to election day as possible, ending not more than three or four weeks before election day; to increase absentee registration opportunities; to reduce residence requirements for voting; to permit new state residents to vote for President; to consider the eighteen-year-old vote; to extend the vote to persons who live on federal reservations; to increase absentee voting opportunities; and to eliminate the poll tax and literacy tests as qualifications for voting.

Almost all of these recommendations have been implemented through a combination of federal and state laws or as the result of Supreme Court decisions. The commission's recommendation that the states should declare a half-day legal holiday on election day has not yet been adopted, though some states have made election day a legal holiday and others have permitted workers time off with leave pay for voting. Although the hours for voting have generally been extended, most states still close the polls at 7:00 p.m. or 8:00 p.m., rather than 9:00 p.m. as recommended by the commission.

Registration Methods

With the exception of North Dakota, each state requires some form of voter registration. The local registrar may be a county clerk, county auditor, city clerk, registrar of voters, or supervisor of elections. Personal registration is available in large jurisdictions during normal business hours and at other specified times. Registration is continuous except for a short period—usually thirty days—just prior to an election, when the registration books are closed so that officials can prepare current precinct lists for use at the polls.

---

[3] See for example, Stanley Kelley, Richard E. Ayres, and William G. Bowen, "Registration and Voting: Putting First Things First," *American Political Science Review*, vol. 61 (June 1967), pp. 359–79. Also, *Administrative Obstacles to Voting*, a report of the Election Systems Project of the League of Women Voters Educational Fund (Washington, D.C.: League of Women Voters of the United States, 1972).

[4] *Report of the President's Commission on Registration and Voting Participation* (Washington, D.C.: U.S. Government Printing Office, 1963).

Most jurisdictions supplement office registration with decentralized location or mobile units. Voters are registered at shopping centers, fire stations, schools, nursing homes, banks, libraries, and other public locations. Some decentralized locations are established on a permanent or semipermanent basis for voter convenience. Mobile registration vehicles are dispatched to register voters at county fairs and other large public gatherings.

Deputy Registrars. Several states authorize deputy registrars who serve with or without pay to register voters wherever they find them. These deputies may function under the general supervision of the local election official or may operate quite independently. In California, a small percentage of the deputies register the vast majority of those who are registered by deputies. Systematic door-to-door voter-registration drives have been conducted in states as diverse as Hawaii, Idaho, and New Jersey.

Until 1974, almost all voter registration methods required the voter to appear in person before a registrar and swear or affirm that the information provided was true. After voter registration by mail was introduced, several states, including Minnesota and Wisconsin, permitted individual citizens, labor unions, political parties, and civic groups to distribute registration forms and to return the completed forms to the appropriate officials. In effect these volunteer efforts served as a deputy registrar system.

Voter Registration by Mail. Registering voters by mail began in 1942 when members of the armed forces were permitted by federal law to register by mail and to vote absentee. Current federal election law extends this opportunity to military spouses and dependents, and to citizens residing overseas.

Proposals for national registration by mail were introduced in Congress in 1971 and in subsequent years. Each year, legislation to establish a national voter registration agency and a system of registration by mail passed one or both houses of Congress but the proposal failed to be enacted in the 92nd, 93rd, or 94th Congresses.

Registration by mail in the states was rare before 1974. Texas used a system of mail registration for many years, but this was originally operated in conjunction with a poll tax and was not widely encouraged until the last two or three years. Kentucky adopted a mail registration law to facilitate reregistration of all electors when a statewide voter registration law was implemented in 1973. A few states permitted absent voters to register by mail under specified conditions.

While Congress debated a national mail registration bill, the states began to pass similar legislation. Minnesota adopted both mail registration and election day registration in 1973. In Maryland, four larger counties and Baltimore City began mail registration the same year. New Jersey's mail registration law took effect shortly before the general election of 1974.[5] By the presidential election of 1976, seventeen states and the District of Columbia had enacted laws which enabled all voters in the state to register by mail. These jurisdictions, which included California, New York, and Pennsylvania, had 47.3 percent of the total national population.[6]

Most states that provide for mail registration permit widespread distribution of mail registration forms by political parties, civic groups, labor unions, and active citizens. Most states also permit those who distribute the forms to return them to the election office but a few states require each registrant to mail or return his own form.

When the registration form is received, the voter is sent a nonforwardable voter notification form advising him that he is registered and providing him with the location of his polling place. If the voter form is returned as nondeliverable, the registration process is suspended until the reason for nondelivery has been ascertained. Ultimately, the voter will be required to furnish evidence that he resides at the address from which he seeks to register.

Although voter registration by mail was widely heralded as a means of increasing voting turnout, the 1976 election did not confirm these expectations. Collectively, the states that introduced or greatly expanded voter registration by mail between 1972 and 1976 suffered a decline in voter turnout of 2 percentage points. States without mail registration voted 54.8 percent of the voting age population in both election years.[7]

Election Day Registration. Long after most states passed laws requiring registration, there were parts of the country in which prior voter registration was not required. As recently as 1970, parts of Iowa, Kansas, Missouri, Minnesota, Nebraska, Ohio, and Wisconsin, and the entire state of North Dakota did not require voter registration. In these areas, voters were presumed to know each other and populations were sufficiently small that the possibility of padding the registration lists and stuffing the ballot box was considered remote. Iowa,

---

[5]A description and evaluation of mail registration may be found in Richard G. Smolka, *Registering Voters by Mail: The Maryland and New Jersey Experience* (Washington, D.C.: American Enterprise Institute, 1975).

[6]*Election Administration Reports*, vol. 6, no. 17 (September 1, 1976). This is a newsletter for election officials edited by Richard G. Smolka and published by Plus Publications, Washington, D.C.

[7]Ibid., vol. 7, no. 1 (January 5, 1977).

Kansas, Missouri, and Nebraska subsequently enacted statewide voter registration requirements.

Only North Dakota, a large part of Wisconsin, a few Ohio jurisdictions, and one county in Minnesota did not have a voter registration requirement in 1976. Minnesota and Wisconsin, however, adopted legislation enabling voters in areas that required voter registration to register at the polls on election day. Town clerks in Maine and county clerks in Oregon are also permitted to register voters on election day, but registration is not normally conducted at the polling places in those two states.

The major difference in procedure between jurisdictions which have election day registration at the polls and those with no registration is that the former maintain a list of registered voters between elections. Procedures to identify unregistered eligible voters at the polls are very similar.

Registration as a Safeguard against Vote Fraud

As a safeguard against fraud, voter registration lists are only as good as the election officials, the political parties, civic groups, and individual voters permit them to be. The basic protection provided by voter registration lies in the advance disclosure and distribution of the list of voters for each precinct. These lists permit political party canvassers to determine whether the persons whose names are on the registry are actually present or absent. Until a very few years ago, Boston and Milwaukee police were required to conduct a door-to-door canvas of every name and address on the registry to ensure that the list was current and accurate. When precinct lists are published by street address, they may reveal unusual numbers of voters at the same address. This may draw the attention of election officials or observers, triggering a pre-election investigation or prompting challenges at the polls to voters who attempt to vote from these questionable addresses. In some jurisdictions, lists of registered voters are posted at the polling places to permit poll watchers, challengers, and supervisory state officials, as well as ordinary voters, to know who is registered in the precinct and from what address, and to challenge anyone whose identity, residence, or qualifications may be doubtful.

The relationship between voter registration and vote fraud is simple and direct. No precinct can report more votes cast than it has registered voters. A precinct which reports an unusually high voter turnout percentage invites suspicion. Persons intent on "stuffing the ballot box" or casting illegal votes screen them by doing so in the name of registered voters. The greater the number of nonvoters on the list, the greater the opportunity to escape detection based upon discrepancies between the number of registered voters and the votes cast.

Voter registration lists may be padded in several ways. Individuals may register under false names, or under their real names but with a false address. Impostors have frequently used the names of persons who have died or moved away. Use of the names of actual persons living or dead is declining because subsequent investigations may establish conclusively the existence of fraud.

An example of how this occurs was revealed by Chicago's Project LEAP, a nonpartisan election watchdog group, during 1977 congressional hearings.[8] According to testimony, the chief investigator of Chicago's Better Government Association checked into a fleabag hotel under the name "James Joyce." He stayed about five minutes and never returned. James Joyce appeared on a subsequent voter registration list and later "voted." Because only two persons—the investigator and a newspaper reporter—knew who James Joyce was, it was clear that the vote was cast fraudulently. Investigations of the 1968 election and 1972 primary elections in Chicago revealed many names of persons who were either falsely registered or falsely voted for those elections.

When attempts are made to falsify voter certificates without using the names of registered voters, the fraud becomes very obvious. For example, the Pennsylvania Crime Commission found that Nikita Khrushchev, Richard Nixon, Gerald Ford, and Lyndon Johnson were recorded as having voted in the same division (precinct) in Philadelphia in April 1976.[9] Another 155 names of prominent entertainers, public officials, and sports figures were also listed on voter certificates in the same precinct. None was listed as a registered voter. When the perpetrator of this fraud exhausted his imagination, he added blank voter certificates until the number of certificates equaled the number of votes cast at the division. The Crime Commission estimated that 38 percent of all votes cast in that division in that election were fraudulent.

If the culprit had attempted to pad the registration rolls with that many names, he could have been detected much earlier, because voter registration lists are widely distributed in each division prior to election day. It would have been extremely difficult to conceal more than a very few fictitious persons from the many interested persons who have an opportunity to study the lists.

---

[8]U.S. Congress, Senate, Committee on Rules and Administration, *Hearings on the Universal Voter Registration Act of 1977*, 95th Congress, 1st session, May 6, 1977.

[9]*Preliminary Report: Voting Irregularities in Philadelphia*, Pennsylvania Crime Commission, March 1977 (mimeo.).

Sometimes vote fraud merely involves voting from the wrong address. A high-ranking fire department official, a labor leader, and an insurance company executive were indicted in 1976 by the San Francisco County grand jury for illegal voting. Each was charged with a felony for voting from city addresses in the 1974 and 1975 city general elections when in fact they lived elsewhere. The indictments followed an investigation of charges of illegal voting by city employees attempting to influence ballot propositions that affected their salaries and pensions. Two such measures passed by narrow margins. After the voting scandal became known, the secretary of state matched the San Francisco voter registration list against records of driver's licenses in the seven surrounding counties and identified 12,000 persons listed on San Francisco rolls who apparently lived outside the city. Election officials announced that all persons identified in this check would be challenged at the polls on June 8 but that "amnesty" would be given to persons who voluntarily removed their names from the list or who did not attempt to vote. Several hundred persons voluntarily removed their names from the voter rolls prior to the June 1976 election.

Use of Voter Registration at the Polls. The usual method of voter identification at the polling place is a signature comparison. The voter is required to sign a ballot application, voter's roster, or other official document. The election day signature is compared with the signature on the voter's original registration card, and, if it appears to match, he is permitted to vote. If not, other proof of identity may be required. In practice, many polling place officials simply do not make the comparison, but the documents are there for later verification if the need arises.

The signature comparison was regarded as a critical "control" mechanism in an internal Justice Department memorandum relating to election day registration. The memorandum stated that the elimination of the "control" signature, which usually appears on the original voter registration card, deprives election officials "of an objective standard by which to judge the qualifications of the persons presenting themselves to vote, while at the same time making proof of election fraud in a criminal case more difficult." [10]

Not all states require a signature check at the polls, and some do not even require identification. The prospective voter merely gives his name and address, and, if the name is listed as given, he is permitted to vote, subject to possible challenge by officials or poll watchers as provided in state law. If identification is required, any of several items

[10] The memorandum, submitted by Peter H. Flaherty, the deputy attorney general, to the Committee on Rules and Administration, U.S. Senate, was printed in the *Congressional Record*, May 10, 1977, p. E 2865.

may be deemed sufficient to establish identity, including a voter registration receipt, driver's license, social security card, library card, credit card, and employer's identification card, depending upon state law and what the precinct officials are willing to accept. In most states, the voter is presumed to be honest, and information is taken at face value unless there is good cause for suspicion.

In some instances, voters whose names are not on the poll list may be permitted to vote, provided they are able to satisfy an administrator or a court that they have preregistered. In other jurisdictions there is no provision for relief. Voting by unregistered persons has been used quite frequently as grounds for election challenges and was an element in the contest of a congressional election from the ninth district of Virginia in 1974.

Use of Voter Registration Statistics

Voter registration statistics vary in quality from jurisdiction to jurisdiction, in relation to the stability of the population, the frequency and thoroughness of the purge process, and the timeliness of reporting. High voter registration does not always mean a jurisdiction is registering many voters. It may merely mean that it is doing a poor job of maintaining a current list of eligible voters. On the other hand, lower voter registration figures may reflect a transient community with a declining population, which has effectively maintained an accurate list of eligible voters.

Statistical analysis of election day registration in Minnesota and Wisconsin requires great care. The Milwaukee County Board of Election Commissioners has published in book form registration and voting statistics for each municipality of the county for 1976. The city also publishes its registration and election returns, and the state has compiled and made available similar statistics in mimeographed form. The problems of interpretation that these statistics present are suggested by Table 1 on page 10.

Not any of the three registered voter or percentage turnout figures is useful for comparison with cities that do not have election day registration. The county report fails to include the 60,415 persons who registered in Milwaukee on election day. The state report shows votes cast for President, but the city report shows the total that came to the polls. Both include thousands of duplicates in registered voters. Officials estimate that about 40,000 of 60,000 election day registrations were made by persons whose names were already on the registry but at a former address.

Table 1
REGISTRATION AND VOTING IN THE CITY OF MILWAUKEE, NOVEMBER 1976

	City Report	County Report	State Report
Registered voters	386,956	326,541	388,088
Number voting	295,636	295,641	284,631
Percentage of registered voters voting	76.4	90.5	73.3

Source: Milwaukee City Board of Election Commissioners, Milwaukee County Board of Election Commissioners, and State Elections Board. Percentages of registered voters voting calculated by author.

Similarly in Minnesota, the total number of *individuals* actually registered cannot be determined by adding the election day registrants to the voters previously registered. Only after the election, and after all the changes of address have been processed, can the total number of persons actually registered be determined.

Voter Turnout. Voter turnout refers to the number of persons who actually come to the polls or who cast ballots in a given election. Not all jurisdictions record or report total voter turnout. For presidential elections, turnout is usually expressed as the number of valid votes cast for President, though an additional 1 to 3 percent of voters either do not vote for President or vote for write-in candidates whose votes are not tabulated. Minnesota and Wisconsin election reports include the number of persons who come to the polls, but independent calculations of voter turnout from these states, when used for comparative purposes, may indicate only the number of votes cast for President or for the highest office on the ballot at a given election. These differences in calculating voter turnout account for most of the differences between various accounts of turnout in the states.

Voting Age Population. The voting age population (VAP) is a base figure used to evaluate both voter registration and voter turnout. Population reports and estimates made by the Bureau of the Census are presumed to be fairly accurate for when the census was taken but are less so for each subsequent year. Nevertheless, for most jurisdictions, there are no better estimates.

Other estimates of voting age population may be developed by state and local government agencies for health or planning or other

10

units of government which have a major interest in population patterns. Each of these is likely to deviate somewhat from the others in the methodology employed and in the population estimate derived.

The voting age population is not the same as the population *eligible* to vote. Aliens, persons convicted of certain crimes, and those who have been judged mentally incompetent are disqualified from voting under the laws of the states. Aliens constitute about 3 percent of the total population but are concentrated in a relatively few cities and states. The number of persons ineligible to vote by reason of conviction for a crime or mental incompetence is not known but probably is less than one-half of 1 percent.

Beginning in 1976, the Census Bureau calculated the voting age population exclusive of aliens. This estimate is probably within 1 percent of the eligible voting population. It differs, however, from previous Census Bureau voting age population estimates for prior presidential election years, which did include aliens. Voter turnout rates for presidential election years prior to 1976 and those which include aliens tend to understate the rate of participation of eligible voters. For 1976, the census estimated voting age population at 150,041,000 according to the former method, but it estimated eligible voters, excluding aliens, at 146,573,000.

Other factors that affect the relationship between voting age population as determined by the census and the number of persons eligible to vote include the presence of persons who reside in an area but do not claim voting residence there. For example, individuals who reside on a military base or a university may be included in some population calculations but may actually claim the right to vote elsewhere. Alaska was placed under the Voting Rights Act because fewer than 50 percent of its voting age population were registered voters, but shortly thereafter the state claimed that it had registered 90 percent of its *eligible* voters. The difference was accounted for by the disproportionate number of military personnel stationed in the state.

The most important consideration in determining the number of persons likely to register in any jurisdiction is not the population but rather the number who move within the jurisdiction. A rapidly growing county has a far greater potential for registration increases than a county with an older and more stable population of the same size. Similarly, a large city that has experienced a population decline, such as Milwaukee, must register many persons who move within its city limits merely to maintain its voter registration level.

From this general discussion of voter registration history and statistics, we turn to the main purpose of this paper—a description and analysis of the process of registering voters at the polls on election day.

The election laws and experiences of Minnesota and Wisconsin described in the following two chapters constitute the basic data for analysis. Although there are similarities, the differences are substantial enough to warrant a separate chapter on each.

2
ELECTION DAY REGISTRATION IN MINNESOTA

Minnesota has long had a reputation for conducting honest and fraud-free elections. Perhaps the best test of this came in 1962 when Karl F. Rolvaag won a closely contested gubernatorial election from the incumbent governor, Elmer L. Anderson, by 91 votes out of 1,257,502 votes cast—a margin of .007 percent—after a recount that took four and one-half months. The recount procedure was as comprehensive and thorough as any recount ever undertaken in the United States. Although more than 800,000 paper ballots were cast, and although the stakes were as high as possible for a state election, allegations of vote fraud were virtually nonexistent.

The authors of a study of that recount said, "The most significant result of this first phase of the recount trial was an indication that under the most acute scrutiny of the two political parties, that there was really no fraud in Minnesota's election and in its system. Fighting fiercely for each vote and checking each ballot intensely (using a magnifying glass in some cases), the Democratic and Republican parties could not find even a trace of fraud." [1]

Minnesota is the nineteenth largest state in the union and in 1970 had a population of 3,805,609. The voting age population of the state, as estimated by the Bureau of the Census, was 2,546,000 in 1972 and had grown to 2,721,000 by 1976.

About one-third of the population lives in the twin cities area of Minneapolis-St. Paul. Hennepin County (Minneapolis) had a 1970 population of 960,080, and Ramsey County (St. Paul) had 476,350.

There are another five counties with populations of over 100,000, but seventy-seven counties have fewer than 50,000. Between 1970 and 1975, the state population increased 2.1 percent, but the two largest

---

[1] Ronald F. Stinnett and Charles H. Backstrom, *Recount* (Washington, D.C.: National Document Publishers, 1964).

Table 2

POPULATION AND REGISTERED VOTERS IN TEN LARGEST MINNESOTA COUNTIES, 1976

	Population		Precincts	Registered Voters Nov. 1976[a]	Average Registered Voters per Precinct
	1970	1976			
County					
Hennepin	960,080	915,603	441	587,234	1,332
Ramsey	476,255	456,006	240	314,482	1,310
St. Louis	220,693	216,220	235	126,947	540
Dakota	139,808	166,754	94	94,841	1,010
Anoka	154,712	186,328	74	71,950	972
Washington	83,003	104,145	66	50,551	766
Olmstead	84,104	87,732	44	44,283	1,006
Stearns	95,400	102,155	88	44,112	501
Blue Earth	52,322	51,734	49	31,087	634
Clay	46,608	46,750	50	25,272	505
State					
Minnesota	3,806,103	3,916,105	3,993	2,111,539	529

[a]Does not include election day registration.

Source: U.S. Department of Commerce, Bureau of the Census, *Current Population Reports*, Series P-25, no. 671, May 1977. Registered voters obtained from *Minnesota General Election, November 2, 1976*, published by Joan Anderson Growe, secretary of state. Number of precincts provided by secretary of state.

counties, Hennepin and Ramsey, lost 44,000 and 20,000 respectively. Declines of 56,000 in Minneapolis and of 30,000 in St. Paul offset growth in the suburban areas of these counties (see Table 2).

Minnesota Election Law

Minnesota's election law regulating federal, state, and municipal elections is contained in Chapters 200 to 211 of the Minnesota Statutes. Special provision is made for town meetings and for school district elections, which are not covered by the election code.

Voters in most of Minnesota have two opportunities each year to cast a ballot. There is a federal and state primary election each even-numbered year, and there is a municipal primary and general election in each odd-numbered year. Special elections and school district elections may be conducted separately and scheduled for other times of the year.

14

Precincts. There are 3,993 precincts in Minnesota, which have from fewer than 10 to more than 4,000 registered voters. Of these precincts, 967 or 24.2 percent of the total, are located within the seven-county twin cities metropolitan area. The average total population of a twin cities precinct is about 2,000 persons, of whom about 1,400 are of voting age. The average population of an outstate precinct—that is, one outside the twin cities area—is approximately 750 persons, of whom about 525 are of voting age (see Table 2). If 10 persons who live in an "unorganized territory," a place which has no township government, request a polling place, they are permitted to have one if there is no polling place within ten miles. There is no legal maximum number of voters who may be registered in a single precinct. The largest precinct, Crystal, W-1, in Hennepin County, recorded 4,566 registered voters and added another 900 election day registrants. At the other extreme, there were precincts with fewer than 10 persons and more than 100 precincts in which fewer than 100 votes were cast in 1976. The rural seventh congressional district contains 1,116 precincts in contrast to the metropolitan third district, which has only 176½ precincts.

Of Minnesota's 3,993 precincts, 74 percent vote on paper ballots. There are 767 precincts with lever voting machines, and another 271 are equipped with punch-card voting devices. Ballots in Minnesota are short. Although the law provides only that there must be one voting machine for each 600 registered voters when the precinct is first formed, local jurisdictions usually make certain that there are sufficient machines to prevent long waiting lines.

The Secretary of State. The secretary of state, the chief election officer of Minnesota, is elected for a four-year term in even-numbered non-presidential election years. The secretary certifies to the county auditors the names of candidates to be voted in more than one county, which are to be placed on the county ballots for primary and general elections. The secretary receives and certifies the form and sufficiency of nomination petitions from such candidates. In addition the secretary approves voting equipment for use in the state.

The secretary also does the following: prescribes the forms to be used for voter registration and other forms, including abstracts, used for reporting the vote; publishes the election code and information bulletins; promulgates rules and regulations governing the conduct of voter registration; and instructs local officials in the conduct of registration and election procedures.

The elections division of the Office of Secretary of State employs four persons full time. The budget for fiscal 1976–1977 was $414,000; it was reduced to $137,318 for fiscal 1977–1978 and increased to $458,830

15

for fiscal 1978–1979. This amount covers all publication expenses, as well as the conduct of elections. The secretary of state publishes the *Legislative Manual*, at a cost of $110,000 every two years, and a variety of information bulletins.

Local Election Officials. The county auditor is responsible for voter registration but may delegate this duty to municipal clerks. In practice, the city clerks in larger municipalities conduct voter registration and compile the registration lists, but the auditors generally retain responsibility for smaller municipalities.

The city clerks are the chief election officers and conduct the election in their respective municipalities. The clerk, rather than the auditor, selects the polling places, recruits the judges, and is responsible for the tally of the votes in the municipality. The auditor compiles the returns for the county from the results obtained from the various municipalities. If the auditor is responsible for registration, he must deliver the list of registered voters to the clerk in time to be used at the polling places on election day. After the election, the registration records are delivered back into the custody of the auditor.

Eligible Voters. An eligible voter in Minnesota is a person who at the time of the election is eighteen or more years of age, is a citizen of the United States, and has resided in Minnesota for twenty days. Residence in Minnesota is considered to be for each person "that place in which his habitation is fixed, without any present intention of removing therefrom, and to which, whenever he is absent, he intends to return."

The section of the law that defines residence, however, contains eleven subsections, which amplify that general principle but make it difficult to determine at any given time what is a residence for voting purposes. For example, one subsection provides that "the mere intention to acquire a new residence, without the fact of removal, shall avail nothing, neither shall the fact of removal, without the intention." A recent court decision ruled that residence for the purposes of voting is based on considerations of physical presence and intent.[2]

Voter Registration

Prior to 1973, only municipalities with a population of 10,000 or more were required to maintain voter registration. In the other areas of Minnesota, where about one-third of the population lived, voters were

---

[2] Bell v. Gannaway 227 N.W. 2d 797 (1975).

permitted to come to the polls, be identified, and vote. This system, long in effect, was administered with a minimum of difficulty and escaped criticism even during the extremely close Rolvaag-Anderson gubernatorial recount in 1962.

In 1973, the law established a statewide permanent voter registration system, which included registration by mail and at the polls on election day. The law required each county auditor to examine the registration list after each calendar year and to remove the names of all voters who had not voted in any election during the four previous calendar years. It gave the secretary of state authority to promulgate rules and regulations necessary to ensure uniform administration of the law. County auditors, rather than municipal clerks, were made responsible for voter registration, although the auditors were permitted to delegate authority to the clerks.

Any county containing no city with a population of 10,000 or more was permitted, by resolution of the county board, to be exempted from the statewide voter registration system. Until 1976, only Pope County had exercised this option, and, after the 1976 presidential election, Itasca County did so. All other counties currently maintain a permanent voter registration system.

When the 1973 law was passed, it provided for state funds to assist the local governments in meeting registration expenses. The legislature originally appropriated $125,000 but was required to pay $800,000 for expenses incurred by the counties, and there are still disputes between the counties and the state regarding payment. When the total cost of voter registration activity became known, the state withdrew its financial support. All registration expenses are currently borne by local governments.

Voter Registration Forms. The Minnesota uniform voter registration form is 6 by 12¾ inches, with blue ink on white 100-pound offset paper. The same form is used regardless whether the voter registers in person, by mail, or on election day. The card is perforated so that three equal-size cards of 6 by 4 inches can be produced. The top, or white, card becomes the original registration; the second section contains instructions to the voter; and the third card, a light blue, becomes the duplicate registration form, which is sent to the polls on election day. The reverse side of the original provides space for the mailing address of the county auditor. The reverse side of the duplicate card provides a record of voting, which is to be completed by election judges each time the registrant votes. The card has a top stub which permits sealing for privacy if it is mailed (see Figure 1).

There is no provision for a declaration of party at the time of voter

Figure 1

MINNESOTA VOTER REGISTRATION FORM

VOTER REGISTRATION CARD

Please type or print in ink — Read instructions before completing

(Left margin, vertical text) ORIGINAL VOTER REGISTRATION CARD

Name _____

              Last   First   Middle

W. _____ P. _____

Legal
Residence_____

(Do not use P.O. box) Street or Route No.   Apt. No. and Rural Box No.

S. D. No. _____

OFFICE USE ONLY

City or Township   County   Zip

Telephone number (optional) _____

Month and Day
of Birth (optional) _____

            Mo.   Day

Previous name (if changed since last registration) _____

Most Recent
Prior Residence _____

         Street or Route No.   Apt. No.

City or Township   County   State   Zip

Your Address at Your
Most Recent Prior Registration _____

          Street or Route No.   Apt. No.

City or Township   County   State   Zip

BE SURE TO CHECK INSTRUCTIONS TO DETERMINE WHETHER YOU ARE QUALIFIED TO REGISTER

I certify that I will be 18 years old on election day and that the above facts are correct. I understand that giving false information to procure a registration is a felony punishable by not more than five years imprisonment and a fine of not more that $5,000.00 or both.

X _____

         DATE   LEGAL SIGNATURE OF VOTER

                             Be sure to sign the blue card.

DO NOT TEAR OFF

INSTRUCTIONS FOR VOTER REGISTRATION

READ CAREFULLY BEFORE REGISTERING

1. Print in ink or type all information requested on the white card.
2. Print or type your legal name — do not use nicknames.
3. Your residence should be that place where you actually live — Post Office Boxes cannot be accepted as legal residence.
4. If your name has been changed through marriage, divorce or decree or order of court since your last voter registration, print or type your former name on appropriate line.
5. Print or type your most recent prior residence. If you have not had a previous residence, print or type "NONE".
6. Address of last previous registration — print or type the address from which you were last registered to vote. If same as last previous address, print or type "SAME". If you have never been registered to vote before, print or type "NONE."
7. After the white card is completed, sign your full name in ink on the appropriate line on *both* the white card and the blue card.
8. The blue card must be signed in ink on the line where it is required, but do not fill in the blue card. It will be typed in by voter registration office.
9. After the white card is completed and both cards are signed, seal using sealing tab attached.
10. Complete the address on the reverse of the white registration card by filling in the name of the county where you reside and the name of the city which is the county seat. Mail or deliver to the office of the county auditor.

(OVER FOR REMAINDER OF INSTRUCTIONS)

Top Sections

18

Figure 1 (Continued)

DUPLICATE VOTER REGISTRATION CARD

VOTER REGISTRATION CARD

Sign this card — DO NOT COMPLETE. The information will be typed by voter registration office.

Name _____

        Last   First   Middle

W. _____ P. _____

Legal
Residence _____

(Do not use P.O. box) Street or Route No.   Apt. No. and Rural Box No.

S. D. No. _____

OFFICE USE ONLY

City or Township   County   Zip

Telephone number (optional) _____

Month and Day
of Birth (optional) _____

      Mo.   Day

Previous name (if changed since last registration) _____

Most Recent
Prior Residence _____

      Street or Route No.   Apt. No.

City or Township   County   State   Zip

Your Address at Your
Most Recent Prior Registration _____

    Street or Route No.   Apt. No.

City or Township   County   State   Zip

BE SURE TO CHECK INSTRUCTIONS TO DETERMINE WHETHER YOU ARE QUALIFIED TO REGISTER

_____ X _____

    DATE   LEGAL SIGNATURE OF VOTER

                (for identification only)

Bottom Section

PLACE

STAMP

HERE

RETURN TO:

Reverse Side—Top Section

19

Figure 1 (Continued)

(OFFICE USE ONLY)	RECORD OF VOTING		
ELECTION DATE	ELECTION DATE	ELECTION DATE	ELECTION DATE

INSTRUCTIONS FOR VOTER REGISTRATION — Continued

An eligible voter — is a person who at the time of any election:

(a) is 18 years of age or older,

(b) is a citizen of the United States and

(c) has resided in Minnesota for 20 days.

The following persons are not eligible voters:

(a) any person who has been convicted of a felony or treason, who has not been restored to his civil rights:

(b) any person who is under guardianship over his person;

(c) any person who is adjudicated to be not mentally competent, and

(d) any person who is not properly registered, in areas that provide for voter registration.

Reverse Side—Bottom Sections

registration. Since primary elections in Minnesota are open, there is no record of the political party primary election in which a voter voted.

Personal and Mail Registration. After the 1973 law took effect, registration was conducted in person at most but not all of the county courthouses and at decentralized locations. In some of the counties where voter registration had not been required previously, no effort was made to register voters prior to election day. Mail registration forms were made easily available at public buildings and were distributed by civic and political groups, many of whom also returned the completed forms to registration officials.

No identification is required for personal or mail registration in Minnesota. The auditor is required by law to send to each registrant a nonforwardable mail notice which indicates the voter's name, address, precinct, and polling place. If the card is returned as nondeliverable, the word *challenged* is affixed to the duplicate registration card. This is the card which is sent to the polling place on election day. The judges must challenge such voters to ensure that they reside at the address indicated. All preregistered voters are required to sign a voter's certificate, which is compared with the signature on the duplicate registration card and approved by the judge.

Election Day Registration. Persons who register on election day are required to complete the same voter registration card, make an oath in the form prescribed by the secretary of state, and provide proof of residence. Minnesota permits any one of five items to be accepted as proof of residence: (1) driver's license or receipt; (2) a nonqualification certificate issued by the Minnesota Department of Public Safety; (3) the oath of a registered voter from that precinct, signed in the presence of a judge, who also signs the oath (see Figure 2); (4) a notice of ineffective registration; and (5) a valid registration certificate in the same precinct.

The first three items are authorized by law and the others have been ruled acceptable by the secretary of state, who is permitted to approve additional documents as proper identification. The election manual prepared by the secretary advised judges that "if there is a question regarding the place of a person's residence, the judges should always take into account the intent of the voter to determine which place the voter considers to be his primary place of residence."

Challenge Procedure. Authorized challengers—or poll watchers, as they are sometimes known—are permitted in the polling place. Challengers, however, may not make a list of voters who have or who have not voted, nor may they handle or inspect any registration files, ballot cards, or lists at the polls.

Figure 2
MINNEAPOLIS PROOF OF RESIDENCE CARD

WHEN IDENTIFICATION IS USED — NOT NECESSARY TO FILL OUT

PROOF OF RESIDENCE — (ELECTION DAY)

I, _____ , swear that I am a registered voter in

_____   _____
              COUNTY   CITY

_____   _____
              WARD   PRECINCT

I personally know that _____
                                         NAME OF PERSON REGISTERING
is a resident of this precinct.

_____
                                  SIGNATURE OF REGISTERED VOTER

Subscribed and sworn to before me

____/____/____   _____
          DATE   SIGNATURE OF ELECTION JUDGE

A challenger must state the specific reason for challenging a voter. Voters may be challenged if they are thought to be someone other than they claim to be, to reside elsewhere than at the address stated, to be under eighteen years of age, or to be under guardianship. If a voter is challenged, the judge administers an oath to the voter and asks relevant questions. If the judge is satisfied that the voter is qualified to vote, the voter may proceed. If the challenged voter fails to answer satisfactorily or to take an oath, he must be denied a ballot. Challenges by poll watchers are almost nonexistent in Minnesota.

Election Day Registration Experience

The first time that election day registration was used, the state paid $25 for each registrar placed in a precinct on election day. In subsequent elections, municipalities made their own determination of whether an additional polling place official was needed for voter registration, and if so, how many. In some municipalities, no registrars were deemed necessary, but in others, such as Bloomington, up to three additional polling place registrars were placed in some precincts.

At the polls, the registration procedure was usually separated from the election process, though both were physically located in the same room. Newly registered persons were required to move to the end of the line for voting and their duplicate registration card was transferred from the registrar to the precinct election judges. Upon approaching the election judge, the election day registrant was required to sign a voter's certificate, which was compared with the registration signature. The judge who authorized the registration could not be the judge in charge of voting.

Minnesota has used election day registration for primary and general elections in all areas since 1974. For this reason, in the 1976 election most officials were experienced and at ease in preparing and handling election day registrations. Nevertheless, the unprecedented numbers and the proportion of voters who registered on election day caused considerable difficulty at the polls. The twenty-five precincts with the largest number of election day registrants in November 1976 are shown in Table 3. There were fifty-eight precincts in which 500 or more voters registered on election day and one in which more than 1,000 persons registered.

In general, election officials believed that the effort of state and local officials and private groups to register voters prior to the 1976 election had registered about 90 percent of the persons likely to vote. They anticipated that only about 10 percent of the voters would register on election day. This estimate proved to be much too low.

The greatest difficulty was reported in precincts with large numbers of voters and especially with a high percentage of election day registrants. If a voter had a driver's license that confirmed his residence within the precinct, processing was quick and routine. If it was necessary to obtain a witness to vouch for the identity or the residence of the voter, or if the election judge refused to accept unauthorized identification, the process took somewhat longer. The lines at polling places placed great pressure on the registrars, and in some instances administrative errors, such as permitting a voter to register and vote in the wrong precinct, occurred. Some voters who had not been adequately identified were permitted to vote because judges would not hold up the line.

Under Minnesota law, a registered voter whose name had been erroneously omitted from the precinct file may be permitted to vote by using an emergency voting card. Most judges simply directed such voters to reregister rather than calling the auditor or city clerk to verify the previous registration. Similarly, many judges did not bother to verify that a prospective registrant had not previously registered from the same address, and there were a substantial number of duplicate registrations.

Table 3

MINNESOTA PRECINCTS WITH LARGEST NUMBERS OF ELECTION DAY REGISTRANTS, 1976

County	Precinct	Total Preregistered Voters	Preregistered Voters Voting	Percent of Preregistered Voters Voting	Election Day Registrants	Total Vote	Percent of Total Vote Cast by Election Day Registrants
Olmstead	Marion	1,668	1,168	70.0	1,068	2,236	47.8
Hennepin	Crystal W-1	4,566	2,804	61.4	900	3,704	24.3
Dakota	Burnsville P-5	4,024	2,461	61.2	785	3,246	24.2
Washington	Forest Lake Twp.	2,002	1,413	70.6	774	2,187	35.4
Hennepin	Maple Grove P-1	3,442	1,961	56.9	768	2,729	28.1
Olmstead	Rochester	1,796	1,332	74.2	760	2,092	36.3
Clay	Moorhead W-3 P-1	2,621	1,356	51.7	740	2,096	35.3
Hennepin	Bloomington P-2	2,696	1,610	59.7	725	2,335	31.0
Blue Earth	Mankato P-11	2,245	899	40.0	713	1,612	44.2
Anoka	East Bethel	1,557	1,326	85.2	710	2,036	34.8
Anoka	Ham Lake	1,848	1,533	82.9	697	2,230	31.3
Ramsey	New Brighton P-2	3,213	2,505	77.9	675	3,180	21.2
Hennepin	Maple Grove P-2	3,312	1,948	58.8	671	2,619	25.6
Ramsey	New Brighton P-3	2,183	1,472	67.4	656	2,126	30.8
Hennepin	Plymouth P-6	3,257	2,013	61.8	651	2,664	24.4
Hennepin	Champlin	2,223	1,340	60.3	636	1,976	32.2
Hennepin	Edina P-16	2,662	1,965	73.8	636	2,601	24.5
Hennepin	Minnetonka W-2 P-4	4,121	3,056	74.2	633	3,689	17.2
Ramsey	Little Canada P-1	1,895	1,202	63.4	631	1,833	34.4
Hennepin	Brooklyn Pk Central P-4	2,277	975	42.8	627	1,602	39.1
Hennepin	Hopkins P-8	1,872	866	46.3	623	1,489	41.8
Dakota	Lakeville P-3	2,185	1,291	59.1	601	1,892	31.8
Clay	Moorhead W-2 P-2	2,466	1,054	42.7	599	1,653	36.2
Clay	Moorhead W-3 P-2	2,359	1,235	52.4	598	1,833	32.6
Hennepin	Bloomington P-16	2,696	1,746	64.8	589	2,335	25.2

Source: *Minnesota General Election, November 2, 1976,* for persons registered as of 7:00 a.m. election day and on election day, and total votes cast in precinct. Other figures derived by author's calculations.

Table 4
ERRORS IN ELECTION DAY REGISTRATION IN BLOOMINGTON, MINNESOTA, NOVEMBER 1976

Voted from wrong precinct	151
No driver's license address	198
Wrong driver's license address	26
No proof submitted	48
Oath signed by nonregistered voter	39
Residence outside Bloomington	2
Total errors	464
Total election day registration	8,193
Percentage of election day registration in error	5.7

Source: Office of the City Clerk, Bloomington, Minnesota.

Table 5
ERRORS IN ELECTION DAY REGISTRATION, MINNEAPOLIS, 1973–76

Election	Election Day Registrations	Faulty Registrations	Percent Faulty
General, 1973	8,371	1,046	12.4
General, 1974	12,004	4,415	35.6
Primary, 1975	1,478	703	47.5
General, 1975	7,268	2,186	30.0
General, 1976[a]	27,302	13,053	47.8

[a]Wards 1 through 9 only. Wards 10 through 13 had not been completed as of May 1977.
Source: Office of the City Clerk, Minneapolis, Minnesota.

Administrative Errors. The cities of Minneapolis and Bloomington kept records of the errors made in processing election day registrations. Minneapolis records include elections since 1973. Bloomington records for 1976 show a much lower error rate than Minneapolis. In Bloomington, only 5.7 percent of the registrations were regarded as faulty in November 1976, compared with almost half of those in Minneapolis. Table 4 shows the number and reason for errors in Bloomington, and Table 5 indicates the error record of Minneapolis

25

from 1973 to 1976. In both municipalities, a card was marked "faulty" if it lacked a specific item required by law or if a voter was permitted to vote in the wrong precinct. In Bloomington, 151 or 1.8 percent of all election day registrants voted in the wrong precinct compared with 1,102 or 4.0 percent in Minneapolis.

Voter Turnout. By any standard, Minnesota led the nation in voter turnout as a proportion of its eligible citizens. Based on voting age population and votes cast for President, Minnesota increased 3.3 percentage points, from 68.4 to 71.7 between 1972 and 1976. Based on 1976 census estimates of *citizens* of voting age, 73.1 percent of eligible citizens went to the polls in Minnesota, though almost 1.5 percent of them did not cast a ballot for President.

A total of 454,147 persons registered to vote on election day. This constituted 22.9 percent of all persons who voted. Many had been previously registered in the city, county, or state. Some of these registrations were duplicates, as noted above, and some were of persons whose previous voter registration could not be located. How many of the election day registrants would have registered without this convenience is difficult to estimate. Election day registration in the ten largest counties, with over half the state's total election day registrants, is shown in Table 6.

Table 6

ELECTION DAY REGISTRATION IN TEN LARGEST COUNTIES OF MINNESOTA, NOVEMBER 1976

County	Total Preregistered Voters	Preregistered Voters Voting	Percent Preregistered Voters Voting	Election Day Registrants	Total Vote	Percent of Vote Cast by Election Day Registrants
Hennepin	587,234	396,204	67.5	93,633	489,837	19.1
Ramsey	314,482	184,913	58.8	45,739	230,652	19.8
St. Louis	126,947	96,079	75.7	19,720	115,799	17.0
Dakota	94,841	63,312	66.8	21,358	84,670	25.2
Anoka	71,950	60,403	83.9	19,080	79,483	24.0
Washington	50,551	37,222	73.6	11,772	48,994	24.0
Olmstead	44,283	30,249	68.3	10,460	40,709	25.7
Stearns	44,112	35,313	80.0	13,243	48,556	27.2
Blue Earth	31,087	20,202	65.0	5,953	26,155	22.7
Clay	25,272	15,236	60.2	6,813	22,049	30.9
MINNESOTA	2,111,539	1,524,539	72.2	454,147	1,978,590	22.9

Source: *Minnesota General Election, November 2, 1976.*

Table 7
ELECTION DAY REGISTRATIONS BY CONGRESSIONAL DISTRICT IN MINNESOTA, NOVEMBER 1976

Congressional District	Preregistered Voters	Election Day Registrants	Percent of Vote by Election Day Registrants	Total Vote	Percent Change in Total Vote 1972–76
1	250,873	62,483	25.2	247,893	+21.0
2	260,853	66,495	25.7	258,620	+18.5
3	310,622	53,092	18.9	280,488	+28.1
4	312,592	45,403	19.8	229,422	+12.0
5	250,252	37,345	19.0	196,774	− 5.8
6	237,390	68,745	26.6	258,047	+19.2
7	225,210	64,697	25.8	251,196	+14.6
8	263,747	55,827	21.8	256,150	+13.8

Source: Office of the Secretary of State.

One expectation of proponents of election day registration was that it would contribute disproportionately to voter turnout in the cities. This does not appear to have occurred, and in fact, some of the evidence points to greater impact in the rural areas of Minnesota. The largest numbers of election day registrants were in the congressional districts farthest from the twin cities. In rural areas, many of these registrants may have been voters living in areas where voter registration was not required in 1972. Also, the figures for some jurisdictions appear to indicate a large number of duplicate registrations. Nevertheless, there appears to be an inverse ratio between population density and election day registration. Part of the explanation lies in the declining population of Minneapolis and St. Paul, but this may not explain fully why the proportion of voters who registered on election day should be lower in those areas. The number of election day registrants as a proportion of voters was also low in the third congressional district, which is the fastest growing district and the one that showed the greatest percentage increase in total vote between 1972 and 1976. This may simply be a result of very successful preregistration efforts in the suburban areas.

Procedures to Detect Fraud. Minnesota relies on one election day and one post-election procedure to detect possible fraud. Before voting, the voter must be identified and his residence address verified, either by a document or by a person willing to vouch for him at the polls. Some time after the election, there is a nonforwardable mail verification of each election day registrant.

The success of the election day safeguard is entirely dependent upon the registration official at the polling place. This official must be capable of ascertaining the identity and residence of each registrant and ensuring that the person lives in the precinct. Most officials reported little difficulty at this step in nonpresidential elections, though there were a high number of errors in registration reported in Minneapolis. The great number of presidential election registrations, however, overwhelmed many registrars at many polling places throughout the state. This produced a relaxed situation, wherein all the proper safeguards were not met, and persons without proper identification or proof of residence were permitted to vote. Some voters were permitted to vote in the wrong precincts. Challenges by poll watchers were rare.

City clerks reported instances where judges refused to accept unauthorized identification, whereupon other voters promptly volunteered to vouch for the registrant, even though their demeanor gave every indication that they did not know the voter or his residence. The secretary of state has interpreted the law to mean that the witness must vouch for the residence of the voter but need not know his name. If a witness recognizes a voter as a resident of an apartment house, that is deemed sufficient.[3] No clerk, auditor, or other election official interviewed during this study knew a single case where a potential voter was challenged and apprehended for attempting to impersonate another voter or for attempting to present counterfeit identification.

Post-Election Audit. Two of the ten largest counties, Olmstead and Stearns, reported that they did not mail out any mail verification forms to check on election day registrants because the procedure was too expensive. The others sent the forms out between November 1976 and May 1977. In most instances, the mail notification forms did not go out before December. The auditor or city clerk assigned available people to process the registrations and the cards were sent out as processed. This processing had not been completed in Minneapolis by May 1977. Clay County completed its cards in April 1977.

Auditors reported that the nondeliverable forms ranged from 1 to 8 percent of all notifications mailed. In each instance, returned forms were treated the same way as mail registration notification forms were handled. The auditor placed a "challenge" on the duplicate registration card, and the voter will be required to submit evidence of residence before being permitted to vote again from that address. Not one of the ten largest counties reported any systematic effort to locate or

---

[3] Personal conversation with the author, May 16, 1977.

28

identify all persons whose cards were returned. Anoka did attempt to telephone 50 percent of the undeliverables, most of whom lived in apartment buildings, but did not continue to attempt to identify persons unknown at the address indicated.

Attempts were also made to contact some of these voters in Dakota County as well. There was nothing in the pattern of undeliverable forms that caused any of the auditors or city clerks in other jurisdictions to believe there might be an organized effort at vote fraud.

Election Contests. Election day registration places responsibility on polling place judges to ensure that voters register and vote only in the correct precinct. Because Minnesota precincts are some times split for municipal districts, it is possible to have one or more variations of the ballot in a single precinct. If many voters are premitted to cast ballots in the wrong precincts or ballots to which they are not entitled, and there is a close election, the results are likely to be contested.

One contest occurred for this reason as a result of the November 1976 election. Merry V. Olson, who apparently lost a Robbinsdale (Hennepin County) city council race by one vote, filed an election contest based on evidence that some who voted in that ward were not residents of the ward. One voter who did not live in the ward, in a sworn statement, admitted voting for the apparent winner. The judge disqualified the vote, creating a 912-912 tie. Merry Olson then won the office on a flip of a coin.

Another contest was filed by State Representative Ron Evans, who lost his seat to David R. Cummiskey by 292 votes, 6,588 to 6,296. In his contest, Evans charged that, in a Mankato precinct, one person had vouched for more than 200 voters without knowing all of them; in addition, he was a challenger and therefore not permitted by law to vouch for voters. The district court held that a person need not know a registrant personally to vouch that the registrant is a resident of the precinct. The court also held his act as a challenger had been unintentional: election officials in the polling place had not informed him that he could not vouch for registrants. The challenger and most of the election day registrants for whom he vouched were college students. The challenger recognized them as students and residents of the precinct, though he did not know each of them by name.

3

ELECTION DAY REGISTRATION IN WISCONSIN

Wisconsin is the sixteenth largest state in the nation, with a population of 4,417,933, according to the 1970 census. The voting age population was estimated to be 2,991,000 in 1972 and had grown to 3,211,000 by 1976. Only Milwaukee, the largest city, and Madison, the state capital, have populations of more than 100,000. The population of the ten largest cities in the state is shown in Table 8.

Wisconsin has had a long history of political reform dating back to the progressive era of Robert La Follette about the turn of the century. The state has been known for clean elections since a voter registration system was put into effect in 1912. At that time an unusual state law provided that three parties, rather than two, be represented on the Milwaukee election board. This provision enabled a Socialist to assist in election administration in Milwaukee. During the decades of the 1920s and 1930s, when other large cities reported major vote fraud scandals, Milwaukee and the rest of Wisconsin were untainted. Patronage is not a major factor in employment and political party identification is somewhat muted by the state's open primary laws.

Wisconsin Election Law

Wards. In Wisconsin, the smallest unit for administering elections is known as a ward rather than a precinct. There are 3,409 wards in the state, of which 491 are in Milwaukee County. The average number of registered voters per ward in the state is 473 and in Milwaukee County is 1,044.

Polling Place Organization. Each ward must have three inspectors on duty and may add others in increments of two, as needed. Other

Table 8

POPULATION, VOTER REGISTRATION, AND TURNOUT IN TEN LARGEST MUNICIPALITIES IN WISCONSIN, NOVEMBER 1976

Municipality	1970 Population (in 000s)	Preregistered Voters	Preregistered Voters Voting	Percent of Total Preregistered Voting	Election Day Registrants	Total Vote	Percent of Vote by Election Day Registrants
Milwaukee	717	327,673	235,221	71.7	60,415	295,636	20.4
Madison	172	106,526	74,844	70.3	12,894	87,738	14.7
Racine	95	47,501	33,340	70.2	6,213	39,553	15.7
Green Bay	87	41,892	31,678	75.6	5,943	37,621	15.8
West Allis	71	40,580	30,631	75.5	4,523	35,154	12.7
Wauwatosa	58	34,578	28,255	81.7	3,125	31,380	10.0
Appleton	57	25,800	21,974	85.2	3,940	25,914	15.2
La Crosse	51	25,815	20,908	81.0	3,801	24,709	15.4
Eau Claire	44	24,785	19,903	80.3	4,203	24,106	17.4
Waukesha	40	21,778	16,097	73.9	4,054	20,151	20.1

Source: Bureau of the Census, *Current Population Reports*, Series P-25, no. 697, May 1977, and State Elections Board. Percentages calculated by author.

election officials are designated ballot clerks or election clerks. Only inspectors, by majority vote, can decide questions which arise during the conduct of voter registration or the count of the vote. Only inspectors are permitted to register voters on election day.

The election inspectors are appointed in February of odd-numbered years from among nominees of the two political parties receiving the greatest number of votes in the ward at the previous general election. The majority party in each ward is entitled to a one-member majority. Many inspectors are paid very low hourly or daily wages, determined by the municipality in which they serve. State law requires only that they be paid a minimum of five dollars a day.

There are elections in Wisconsin every year. In even-numbered years a federal and state primary and general election is held in the fall. The presidential primary election is held in the spring of every presidential election year. Nonpartisan elections are held in the spring of odd-numbered years. The frequent elections usually ensure that Wisconsin voters will have a relatively short ballot.

Voter registration is nonpartisan and primary elections are open. At a partisan primary election, each voter is given the ballots of all political parties but may vote for the candidates of only one. Whether the vote is on paper ballot or machine, there is no way to determine in which party primary any individual voter has voted.

State Elections Board. Elections in Wisconsin are conducted under the general supervision of the state elections board. The board, which was created by law in 1973 and came into being in July 1974, is composed of eight persons appointed by the governor. Of these, one is designated by and serves at the pleasure of the governor. The other seven members serve two-year terms. One member is designated by each of the following: the chief justice of the supreme court, the majority and minority party leaders of each house of the legislature, and the chief officer of each political party whose candidate for governor received at least 10 percent of the vote in the most recent election.

The state elections board is generally responsible for voter registration, the conduct of elections, and the administration of the campaign finance laws. The major portion of the workload of the state elections board deals with campaign finance laws. The board prepares forms to be used by candidates and committees, prescribes procedures to be followed, publishes information pamphlets and manuals, receives the completed forms, makes them available for public inspection, and examines the reports for accuracy. In addition, the board audits every report to determine completeness, accuracy, and compliance with the law. The board also conducts field audits on a sample basis, consisting of a detailed physical examination of all supporting records of candidates, committees, and groups at the residence or business of the respective campaign managers.

The board is empowered to assess forfeitures, to bring civil actions to require forfeitures, and to sue for injunctive relief to compel compliance with the act. It also publishes a detailed report, containing the total amounts contributed and spent and an analysis based upon breakdowns by elective offices and contributions by specific groups, as well as other factors deemed to be important public information.

The state elections board also receives nomination papers for candidates for state and judicial offices, reviews all petition signatures presented in support of a state or judicial candidate or question, and determines whether the signatures are filed in a timely manner, are proper in form, and are sufficient in number to support a candidate or question for a position on the ballot.

The board prescribed the forms, developed procedures and promulgated regulations necessary to ensure implementation of the voter registration law during June 1976. It conducted a series of three major voter registration workshops for local election officials at Eau Claire, Green Bay, and Oconomowoc and maintained a continual educational and information program for the balance of the year.

The board has ten full-time employees, including full-time legal counsel, and two to six part-time employees who work as needed. Audit services are provided by an auditor assigned to the board by the legislative audit division. Budget for the state elections board for fiscal 1976–1977 was $250,000.

Local Officials. Voter registration and the conduct of elections in Wisconsin are the responsibility of the municipal or city clerk except in Milwaukee where a city and a county board of election commissioners has been created by state law. There are nineteen municipalities including the city of Milwaukee in Milwaukee county. The county board canvasses all elections, verifies the legality of nomination papers, prints ballots and maps, and prepares a statistical booklet after each election and registers city of Milwaukee electors. The Milwaukee City Board of Election Commissioners conducts voter registration and elections. Each municipality in Milwaukee County maintains its own list of voter registration, and there is a duplicate master list of registered voters for the county.

Outside Milwaukee County, county clerks are responsible for preparing ballots, but municipal clerks are responsible for voter registration and the conduct of elections.

Voter Registration

In 1864, the first Wisconsin voter registration law was passed to permit municipalities to compile the list of voters prior to each general election. No person could vote unless his name appeared on a registration list. In 1912 the city of Milwaukee changed from this periodic registration system to a system of permanent voter registration, and in 1927 a permanent voter registration system was established for municipalities of over 5,000 population. The permanent registration system provided that a voter's name would remain on the list unless he moved or failed to vote within a two-year period.

Governor's commissions to study registration and voting were created in 1964 and again in 1971, but the law on the books since 1927 remained essentially unchanged until 1975.

In 1972, the task force of voter registration and elections established by Governor Patrick J. Lucey recommended that a universal voter registration system be established.[1] The major features of the system recommended included:

- mandatory statewide voter registration
- a master voter registry list to be compiled and maintained by the state's election officer
- local government responsibility for active recruitment of potential registrants through door-to-door and mail canvasses
- use of high schools as permanent registration locations
- a complete mail canvass of every municipality by its municipal clerk every four years prior to the first election of that year
- a provision that the challenger, rather than the challenged voter, appear before the clerk and election board in registration disputes

The Wisconsin law, which became effective July 1, 1976, and did not apply to the presidential primary held earlier in the year, retained optional voter registration for communities of 5,000 or less. The law introduced registration by mail and election day registration to all communities which require voter registration. Of 1,850 communities, only 245 have voter registration, but about two-thirds of the total population of the state reside in these communities. About 125 of the 245 are communities with populations of less than 5,000 which have decided to establish permanent voter registration.

Eligible Voters. Wisconsin permits U.S. citizens to vote if they are eighteen years of age or older on election day and have been residents

[1] Wisconsin Legislative Reference Bureau, *Recent Changes in Voter Registration*, Informational Bulletin 75-1B-7, November 1975.

35

for ten days of the election district or ward. Residence is defined as the place where the voter's habitation is fixed "without any present intent to move, and to which, when absent, he intends to return." As in Minnesota, the Wisconsin law states that "neither an intent to acquire a new residence without removal, nor a removal without intent, shall affect residence." Wisconsin law also specifically provides that student status shall not be a consideration in determining residence for the purpose of establishing voter eligibility.

The regular registration period closes at 5:00 p.m. on the second Wednesday before the election. Electors may register at the municipal clerk's office during normal business hours throughout the year. Clerks may establish other registration sites in public areas and may appoint anyone as a special registration deputy. Citizens may volunteer to be appointed as special registration deputies.

Each city, town, or village having registration must have forms available to register voters by mail. Any resident of a municipality has a right to request a reasonable number of forms, and the municipal clerk is prohibited from refusing such requests without explanation. Wisconsin law permits individuals to distribute registration forms without restriction, but all such forms filled out by registrants must be witnessed by two other adults. These witnesses must live in the registrant's ward or aldermanic district but they need not be registered voters. The prepaid registration form must be returned to the clerk by mail and postmarked no later than the close of registration.

Registration is also required at all public high schools in Wisconsin and may be established at private high schools at the request of the principal. Students seventeen years of age or older who will be eighteen by the day of the election are permitted to register.

The most significant change made by the new law provided for registration at the polling places on election day. It permitted citizens to register and vote only at the polling place in the ward or aldermanic district of their residence, provided they had proper identification or could be identified by a witness. The witness, who need not be a registered voter, must reside in the same ward or aldermanic district as the registrant.

Proof of Residence. The law provides that an election day registrant must prove his identity and residence by a Wisconsin driver's license, a Wisconsin identification card, or any other proof prescribed by rule of the board. The state elections board adopted a rule to include "a current library card, a current university, college or technical institute identification card together with a current university, college or technical institute fee card bearing the student's local address,"[2] and any other documentation acceptable to the election inspectors, as acceptable proof of identity or residence. If a prospective voter does not have any proof of residence, any person who resides in the same ward or election district may vouch for the accuracy of the statement by witnessing the affidavit. The person who vouches for a registrant need not be a registered voter but may be asked to show proof of residence. The address of the witness is not recorded on the affidavit.

Registration Forms. In contrast to Minnesota, Wisconsin municipalities are permitted to design and to use their own registration forms, provided they contain the information required by state law. Many jurisdictions have separate forms for personal, mail, and election day registration because there are different requirements for each. When registration is in person, the card is signed by a registration officer. Registration by mail requires the signatures of two witnesses who are residents of the elector's ward or aldermanic district, and registration on election day may require the signature of a witness. Examples of the three types of registration cards are shown in Figure 3.

The city of Madison, by contrast, uses a single form for all registrations. The form is a card 12 by 6 inches, divided into three parts by perforations. The top portion is an authorization to cancel a previous registration and is designed in the form of a post card ready to be mailed. The second portion contains instructions to the voter. The third portion is the original voter registration card, which provides space for all signatures needed, regardless of the method of registration. It also requests the social security number of the voter, though registration is not denied if the number is not furnished. The reverse side is addressed to the city clerk, and postage is paid by the board.

Since 1912, Wisconsin registration procedures have requested only a minimum amount of information, and this was not changed when mail and election day registration were introduced. A registrant is required to provide only his name, address, birth date, and birth place. Naturalized citizens must provide the date and place of naturalization. The form does not require length of present residence, a former residence address, or any type of personal identification.

Challenges. Challenges to registered voters may be made prior to election day, but the challenger must appear in person before the municipal clerk to file the challenge. On election day, inspectors are required by law to challenge the persons whom they know or suspect

---

[2] Section on Election Board, Wisconsin Administrative Code, 3.04. Rule adopted July 6, 1976.

Figure 3

MILWAUKEE VOTER REGISTRATION FORMS

REGISTRATION CARD – CITY OF MILWAUKEE

DATE _____

NAME _____

RESIDENCE _____

ALD.
DIST. _____ WD. _____

BIRTH DATE _____ BIRTHPLACE _____

NATURALIZATION (If foreign born)	DATE	CITY	STATE

STATE OF WISCONSIN
Milwaukee County

I hereby swear (or affirm) that I am a citizen of the United States, that on the day of the next election I shall be at least 18 years of age, and shall have resided in the state of Wisconsin, and in the ward 10 days preceding said election, and that I am legally qualified to vote.

SIGNATURE _____

WE THE UNDERSIGNED WITNESSES, RESIDENTS OF THE ELECTOR'S WARD OR ALDERMANIC DISTRICT, SUBJECT TO PENALTIES OF S. 12.60, WIS. STATS. FOR FALSE STATEMENTS CERTIFY THAT THE STATEMENTS APPEARING HEREON ARE TRUE TO THE BEST OF OUR KNOWLEDGE.

NAME _____ ADDRESS _____
(Witness Signature)

NAME _____ ADDRESS _____
(Witness Signature)

Mail Voter Registration Form

REGISTRATION CARD – CITY OF MILWAUKEE

DATE _____

NAME _____

RESIDENCE _____

ALD.
DIST. _____ WD. _____

BIRTH DATE _____ BIRTHPLACE _____

NATURALIZATION (If foreign born)	DATE	CITY	STATE

I do solemnly swear or affirm to the best of my knowledge, I am a qualified elector, having resided at the above address for at least ten days immediately preceding this election, and that I am not disqualified on any ground from voting, and I have not voted at this election.

SIGNATURE _____

WITNESS _____
(Required when offered proof of residency is not accepted)

Subscribed and sworn to before me: INSPECTOR _____

Election Day Voter Registration Form

Figure 3 (Continued)

REGISTRATION CARD — CITY OF MILWAUKEE

DATE _____

ALD.
DIST. _____ WD. _____

NAME _____

RESIDENCE _____

BIRTH DATE _____

BIRTHPLACE _____

STATE OF WISCONSIN }
  Milwaukee County   } ss.

I hereby swear (or affirm) that I am a citizen of the United States, that on the day of the next election I shall be at least 18 years of age, and shall have resided in the state of Wisconsin, and in the ward 10 days preceding said election, and that I am legally qualified to vote.

_____
Signature of Elector

_____
Registration Officer

In-Person Voter Registration Form (front)

EC-6

ADDITIONAL QUESTIONS TO BE ANSWERED

CERTIFICATE OF NATURALIZATION? _____

WHERE ISSUED _____

DATE ISSUED _____ PETITION NO. _____ SERIAL NO. _____

PRINTED BY BOARD OF ELECTION COMMISSIONERS — CITY OF MILWAUKEE

(back)

are not qualified electors. The challenge consists of an oath administered to the voter, followed by a series of questions to determine
whether that elector is qualified. If a voter wishes to challenge the
qualifications of another voter, the challenger is placed under oath and
is required to answer questions relating to the qualifications of the
challenged voter. After the challenger has established the grounds for
the challenge, the challenged voter is then required to take an oath and
answer relevant questions. The entire burden of proof is on the challenger, and contradictions are resolved in favor of a challenged voter
willing to support his statements with the oath. In practice, a challenge
to a voter by an inspector or another voter in Wisconsin is very rare.

Purges. Following each general election, the clerk must send an address verification card to each registered voter who has not voted
during the preceding two years. If the card is returned by the postal
service, the registration is cancelled. Otherwise, the registered voter is
presumed to reside at the same address and the registration is retained.

In addition, a municipal clerk may conduct door-to-door and mail
registration canvasses at any time. The canvasses must be conducted in
a uniform manner throughout the municipality and may be used to
add, as well as to delete, names from the roster.

From 1912 until about 1969, prior to each election the city of
Milwaukee conducted a door-to-door police check of the roster of
registered voters. For many years, a precinct roster was posted in
several places in the precinct before the election to permit voters to
ascertain whether they were listed and to deter fraudulent registration.
The time and expense required to conduct the police check contributed
to its demise. For many years, it was widely regarded as means of
ensuring a clean and current election roster in Milwaukee, when other
cities were experiencing wholesale voter fraud.[3]

Election Day Registration Experience

Polling Place Procedure. To provide for election day registration,
separate tables were set up in wards where a large number of election
day registrants were anticipated. In some jurisdictions, however, no
additional election officials were added and a single line was used to
process registration and voting. This contributed to delays in processing preregistered voters. In areas where registration was separated
from voting, the polling place operated somewhat more smoothly.

---

[3]Joseph P. Harris, *Registration of Voters in the United States* (Washington, D.C.: Brookings
Institution, 1934) pp. 274–84.

After the election day registrant completed his affidavit, it was initialed by the inspector and then carried by the registrant to the election clerk, who accepted the affidavit and added the name of the registrant to a supplementary poll list. No original record of registration was retained by the inspector.

In most jurisdictions, inspectors made no attempt to solicit information about a former address or former registration from the election day registrant. To do so would have been more than the law required and would have contributed to even greater delays at the polls. Many "new registrations" were in fact changes of address or duplications, and there has been no systematic attempt to determine how many are in either category. Thus, in Wisconsin as in Minnesota, it is impossible to determine how many individuals are actually registered by adding election day registration to preregistration totals.

The names of persons who are registered on election day are entered on a supplementary poll list, which is forwarded to the city clerk after the close of the polls. In Madison, to facilitate registration at the polls, inspectors were requested to send the cards to the city clerk, and the supplementary list was compiled after the election. Figure 4 shows a supplementary list from Madison (note that although the law requires proper names to be used, the names of Jim, Jack, and Chris are found in the list).

Difficulties. The state elections board asked municipal clerks for comments about how the election day registration worked at the polls and for suggestions for improvement. The responses, obtained from 180 of the 245 places that conducted registration, were classified as follows:[4]

- There were long lines of irate and disgusted voters.
- People were discouraged from voting because of lines and confusion.
- Voters who registered before elections were penalized.
- Voters were unaware of proper polling place.
- Voters were registered in the wrong wards.
- There were considerable instances of multiple registrations (10 percent in Kenosha, 30 percent in Manitowoc).
- There were suspicions of multiple voting in many communities.
- There were many problems with changes of address causing multiple registrations.
- It was difficult to check identification on election day.
- There was inadequate proof of residence.

[4]Mimeographed summary sheet, State Elections Board, November 17, 1976.

Figure 4

MADISON, WISCONSIN SUPPLEMENTARY
VOTER REGISTRATION LIST

7-2	ADDITIONS TO THE OFFICIAL POLL LIST			
VOTER SLIP NO.	**LAST NAME**	**FIRST NAME**	**MI**	**STREET ADDRESS**
986	Amato	Geri	M	722 Cabot Lane
283	Balkin	Judith	L	4905 Tokay Blvd
284	Balkin	Kenneth	R	4905 Tokay Blvd
1253	Clyman	Jody	D	4829 Sherwood Rd.
246	Doudna	Joyce	M	5213 Odana Rd.
882	Ellingson	Jim	B	5001 Woodburn Dr.
975	Harris	Donna	E	614 Constitution Lane
1291	Hess	Jennifer	J	4501 Odana Rd.
233	Koller	Patricia	J	4802 Odana Rd.
362	Hixson	Delores	Y	4401 Rolla Lane
1188	Kreul	William	C	4814 Woodburn Dr.
970	Mortensen	Jack	W	649 Orchard Dr.
1135	Schmitz	Jeffrey	S	489 Woodside Terrace
881	Srb	John	A	5010 Woodburn Dr.
923	Staley	Philip	R	613 Orchard Dr.
1293	Thorson	Alice	A	726 Odana Lane
658	Turner	Ann	J	609 Orchard Dr.
1019	Winzenried	Mark	S	5224 Odana Rd.
575	Zwettler	Chris	J	4605 Odana Rd.
496	McCreary	Mary/ Nancy	J	5309 Coney Weston
1268	T Roberts	James	H	629 Constitution Lane
654	Swennes	Stephen	R	4502 Teavis Terrace

REGISTRATION NO. (This is a perm. no. to be entered only when given by City Clerk)	Corrected By	New Regis- tration	Address Change	Mili- tary
197917		X		
197918		X		
197919		X		
197920		X		
197921		X		
197922		X		
197923		X		
197924		X		
197925		X		
197926		X		
197927		X		
197928		X		
197929		X		
197930		X		
197931		X		
197932		X		
197933		X		
197934		X		
197935		X		
065393			X	
124301			X	
180675			X	

- It was difficult to find witnesses in lieu of proof of residence.
- Address verification was difficult on election day.
- Ballots and registration forms ran out.
- Inspectors were unfamiliar with boundaries.
- Poll workers were too rushed to take breaks and lunch and dinner periods.
- Poll workers would refuse to work under similar circumstances in future.
- Election costs were substantially increased.
- Clerk's office duties were substantially increased.
- The electoral process has been degraded by encouraging fraud.
- Voters are encouraged to register on election day rather than before.

Many of these difficulties were attributed to the unexpectedly high election day registration in the larger areas. Officials observed that primary election registration gave them no indication of the number of voters to expect on election day (see Table 9). Several did observe that there was no last minute rush of registrants as there had been in prior registration years, but this was attributed to the availability of mail registration and to extensive activity by political and civic groups to

Table 9
ELECTION DAY REGISTRATION IN THE TEN LARGEST MUNICIPALITIES IN THE PRIMARY AND GENERAL ELECTION OF 1976

Municipality	Primary	General	Ratio of General to Primary
Milwaukee	3,622	60,415	17:1
Madison	3,985	12,894	3:1
Racine	455	6,213	14:1
Green Bay	601	5,943	10:1
West Allis	155	4,523	29:1
Eau Claire	183	4,203	23:1
Waukesha	313	4,054	13:1
Appleton	318	3,940	12:1
La Crosse	476	3,801	8:1
Wauwatosa	127	3,125	25:1

Source: State Board of Elections, Survey of Voter Registration at Polling Places, undated mimeographed report.

register voters. Neither the state nor the local government officials advertised the availability of election day registration until after the close of regular registration, thirteen days before the election. Officials reported that they subsequently learned of party and candidate activity advising voters of the election day registration procedure. Part of the election day turnout was attributed to the distribution of this information well in advance of the close of registration.

Voter Turnout. Wisconsin voter turnout has been above the national average for the past 102 years. Between 1972 and 1976, the national average as a percentage of the voting age population declined from 55.6 to 54.4, but in Wisconsin the turnout increased from 62.0 to 65.5, a gain of 3.5 percentage points. Only Minnesota, Utah, and North Dakota voters went to the polls in greater proportions than Wisconsin voters. During that same four years, the state voting age population increased 7.5 percent, but the total votes cast increased by 13.5 percent. Of the 2,104,175 total votes cast in Wisconsin in November 1976, 210,600, or 10 percent, were cast by persons who registered at the polls. This 10 percent does not include persons who lived in the 1,600 places that did not require voter registration.

In Milwaukee, the vote increased from 269,000 in 1972 to 295,000 in 1976, despite a decline in population of about 40,000 during that period. The 60,415 persons who registered in Milwaukee on election day cast 20.4 percent of the city's ballots. The total number of election day registrations and the proportion of election day registrations as a percentage of the total votes cast in the ten largest municipalities in Wisconsin are shown in Table 8.

In an attempt to assess the impact of election day registration on voter turnout, Gerald J. Ferwerda, executive secretary of the state elections board, compared turnout in municipalities without voter registration to those with voter registration. He selected one municipality of each type from fifty-three counties and included Milwaukee and Kenosha counties, though there were no communities in their respective counties that did not have voter registration. The results are shown in Table 10.

Ferwerda concluded that "there was little or no visible effect" on voter turnout from election day registration. "Both sets of municipalities showed increases for each municipality in both sets and showed similar patterns between sets."[5] He further concluded that the increase in voter turnout in 1976 was due to "other phenomena and not related to the registration process or the changes in the registration process implemented in 1976."

---

[5] Memorandum from Gerald J. Ferwerda to election board members, March 22, 1977.

Table 10

PERCENTAGE INCREASE IN VOTER TURNOUT IN SELECTED MUNICIPALITIES, 1972–76

	Municipalities with Registration (55)	Municipalities without Registration (53)
0-10 percent	26	16
11-20 percent	20	20
21-30 percent	6	10
31-40 percent	3	6
41-50 percent	0	1

Source: Memorandum from Gerald J. Ferwerda to election board members, March 22, 1977. Table created from data by author.

Ferwerda did not compare voter turnout with voting age population or with total population in any area. Because substantial increases also occurred in areas without voter registration, not all of Wisconsin's 3.5 percentage point increase can be attributed to election day registration. Despite this, it should not be concluded that election day registration made no impact in the city of Milwaukee. Between 1972 and 1976 the population in the city declined by about 7 percent, but the turnout increased by more than 9 percent.[6] The turnout caught the most astute political observers by surprise, including those election officials who had long been familiar with the city's voting history.

Fraud Prevention. Wisconsin provides two safeguards against voter fraud by persons who register on election day. At the polling place, the election day registrant must offer identification or obtain the signature of a witness to attest to his qualifications. After the election, a nonforwardable registration notification must be mailed to each election day registrant. An example of this form is shown in Figure 5. If a card is returned as nondeliverable, this information must be turned over to the district attorney. The law does not prescribe what steps the district attorney should take.

Interviews with many city clerks and district attorneys have failed to identify a single voter who was denied an opportunity to vote if the voter claimed a residence within the precinct. Although the driver's license was reportedly the most common means of identification,

[6]The 1970 census reported Milwaukee population at 717,372. The city's population was estimated at 665,796 for mid-1975 by the Census Bureau. U.S. Department of Commerce, Census Bureau, press release, April 14, 1977.

Figure 5

VOTER NOTIFICATION FORM, WAUWATOSA, WISCONSIN

OFFICIAL VOTER ADDRESS VERIFICATION

The official voter registration list shows that you are registered to vote by the name and address appearing on the front of this card. If either the name or address appearing on the front of this card is incorrect, please contact this office in person or by mail. Improper registration may result in your being denied the right to vote.

Office of Clerk _____ **J. R. NEUMAN, CITY CLERK** _____

Clerk's Address _____ **7725 WEST NORTH AVENUE** _____

_____ **WAUWATOSA, WISCONSIN 53213** _____

You are registered to vote in ward _____, aldermanic

district _____ located at _____

_____

---

election day registrants offered inspectors library cards, utility bills, letters, and even their own names written on a plain piece of paper. Inspectors generally adopted the position that if the voter was willing to sign an affidavit that the information given was accurate, that was sufficient. Individuals were reported to have vouched for persons without identification whom they apparently did not know, simply to get the line moving, but the extent of this practice could not be determined. The affidavit does not require a witness to list his address. No records were maintained to indicate what type of identification was presented to the inspector either by the registrant or by a witness.

After the election, city clerks mailed nonforwardable notification forms to election day registrants. Among the ten largest jurisdictions, between 1 and 6 percent of all forms were returned as not deliverable. Some city clerks succeeded in locating the registrants by telephone to verify the residence address. Other city clerks merely forwarded all returns to the district attorney. Most jurisdictions had completed the process of mailing the cards before the end of November.

The district attorneys who received the cards from the various municipal clerks in their counties did not consider verification of registrants a high priority duty. In some counties, such as Outagamie, a check was made on all names and addresses by the end of January, but

47

in other counties, the process took a little longer. Some district attorneys attempted to verify by telephone; others authorized a police check of the residence, when time permitted; and, in one county, a sample survey was made because the number of returns, 245, was smaller than the difference in any election and could not affect the outcome. In each county, there were some persons who could not be found, but no district attorney considered this grounds for believing that vote fraud had occurred, much less evidence on which to base a prosecution. In Milwaukee County, District Attorney E. Michael McCann responded to complaints of vote fraud. He also conducted an investigation of about 500 of the approximately 2,800 persons whose voter notification forms had been returned by the postal service as undeliverable, particularly in transient areas where vote fraud was believed to be more likely. The investigation was still being conducted six months after the election, and no results had been made available to the public.

The Justice Department in the Eastern District of Wisconsin conducted an extensive investigation into allegations of vote fraud. They pursued leads provided by the political parties or newspaper reports that some voters did not live at the address indicated or that there was no such address. They noted that such apparent irregularities are inconclusive evidence of fraud, particularly when they are developed weeks or months after election day. In a January 27, 1977, letter to Representative Robert W. Kasten (Republican, Wisconsin), Thomas E. Martin, assistant U.S. attorney wrote:

> To date, no one has been able to substantiate or corroborate in any manner allegations of organized voting fraud. No one has produced a single license plate number, a positive identification of a suspicious registrant; no one has directed our attention to any registration form in particular; no one has identified or alleged that certain identified persons handed out money or threatened employees; no one has come forward who was a witness to a conversation indicating knowledge of a vote fraud scheme. Many people have suspicions and many people have shared their speculation with us, but to date, no one has provided any concrete evidence to substantiate their allegations and suspicions.

Although the state board of elections placed vote fraud on its agenda for three consecutive months, no one took advantage of the opportunity to register specific complaints with the board.

Shortly after the election, Representative William A. Steiger (Republican, Wisconsin), announced that three students told him they had voted twice in Madison. Steiger was unwilling to release the names of the students either to the city clerk or to the district attorney, and there was no further investigation of this incident.

Election Contests. Following the November 1976 general election, the American Independent Party and the U.S. Labor Party attempted to get a recount of the presidential election results in Milwaukee County. They claimed that there had been widespread voter fraud in the city. The recount request was denied by the county board of election commissioners, who ruled that only a candidate, not a political party, was entitled to ask for a recount. The board's decision was then upheld by the circuit court. An appeal was made to the state supreme court, which refused to order a recount in December because the election had already been certified when the case came to the court. The parties also filed a misdirected request for a recount with the state board of elections, rather than the state board of canvassers. This technically deficient effort also failed.

The extent to which a recount procedure would have inquired into false registrations is uncertain. If specific charges had been made against named voters or other persons, these could have been investigated. Otherwise, a recount would have consisted of a retabulation of the votes shown on voting machines, which had been impounded pending the court decision. There was no recount or election contest conducted for any office following the November 1976 general election.

4
EFFECTS OF ELECTION DAY VOTER REGISTRATION

What are the effects of election day registration on prior registration, voter turnout, potential for fraud, administration of elections, and election contests? The experience of Minnesota and Wisconsin provides some tentative answers to some of these questions but more conclusive answers must await several elections and similar experiments in states with different political cultures and traditions.

Preregistration of Voters. Election officials in Minnesota and Wisconsin agreed that the opportunity for election day registration greatly reduced the number of voters who registered prior to election day. Perhaps the most affected were voters who were already registered at a former address. Estimates of such voters ranged from one-third to two-thirds of all election day registrations. Unfortunately, few jurisdictions maintained records to confirm these estimates, and in Wisconsin, the registration form did not request a former address or past registration information.

In Minnesota, 1,524,443 preregistered voters voted. If no others had voted, Minnesota turnout would have declined by 217,209 votes between 1972 and 1976. This decline, from 68.4 percent to 56.0 percent of the voting age population, would have been too large to be consistent with the national pattern and with Minnesota's long record as a high turnout state. Therefore it may be concluded that a substantial proportion of Minnesota election day registrants may have already been registered or would have registered earlier if so required.

In Wisconsin, the pattern is not quite so clear. The votes of preregistered voters and persons living in places without registration constituted 58.9 percent of the voting age population. If no others had voted, Wisconsin turnout would have declined only 3.1 percentage points from 1972. A decline of this magnitude was not uncommon among the

Table 11

VOTES CAST FOR PRESIDENT IN MINNEAPOLIS, ST. PAUL, AND MILWAUKEE, 1972 AND 1976

	Votes Cast for President 1972	Percent of State Vote	Votes Cast for President 1976	Percent of State Vote	Percent Vote Increase 1972–76	Population Change 1970–75
MINNESOTA						
Minneapolis	195,842	11.2	198,233	10.2	1.2	−12.9
Rest of Hennepin Co.	247,516	14.2	285,145	14.6	15.2	+ 2.0
Total Hennepin Co.	443,358	25.4	483,378	24.8	9.0	− 4.6
City vote percentage of county vote	44.1		41.0			
St. Paul	135,151	7.7	136,761	7.0	1.2	− 9.8
Rest of Ramsey Co.	74,800	4.3	91,306	4.7	22.0	+ 6.0
Total Ramsey Co.	209,951	12.0	228,067	11.7	8.6	− 4.3
City vote percentage of county vote	64.3		60.0			
All other counties	1,088,343	62.5	1,238,144	63.5	13.8	+ 7.4
State Total	1,741,652		1,949,589		11.9	+ 2.9
WISCONSIN						
City of Milwaukee	260,652	14.1	284,896	13.5	9.3	− 7.2
Rest of Milwaukee Co.	156,325	8.4	171,849	8.2	9.9	+ 0.3
Total Milwaukee Co.	416,977	22.5	456,745	21.7	9.5	− 4.0
City vote percentage of county vote	62.4		62.4			
All other counties	1,435,913	77.5	1,647,430	78.3	14.7	+ 6.0
State Total	1,852,890		2,104,175			

Source: Office of Minnesota Secretary of State; Milwaukee County Board of Election Commissioners; U.S. Census Bureau, *Current Population Reports*, Series P-25, Nos. 671 and 697, May 1977.

states in 1976. It would appear that more persons in Wisconsin than in Minnesota might not have voted without the opportunity to register on election day.

Nevertheless, registration opportunities were readily available in both states through vigorous party, candidate, and civic group activity with mail registration forms, and the many decentralized personal voter registration locations available in both states. Further, the close of registration in Minnesota and Wisconsin, twenty and thirteen days prior to an election, is nearer to the election date than in most states, where thirty days is the norm. If, given the opportunities and the deadlines in Minnesota and Wisconsin, more than 20 percent wait until election day to register, it would appear probable that election day registration would be even higher in states with a lower proportion of preregistered voters and less opportunity to register. This does not mean that election day registration will dramatically increase turnout, but rather that a high percentage of those who turn out will register on election day.

Turnout. Election day registration has produced mixed results since it was first introduced in Minnesota in 1973. Voter turnout actually declined between 1970 and 1974 by 113,000, even though election day registration had been introduced and eighteen-year-olds had been enfranchised in the interim. In 1976, however, voter turnout increased by more than 200,000 from 1972, almost 12 percent, though population had increased only about 3 percent during the same time.

Despite substantial population declines in the twin cities of Minneapolis and St. Paul, there were slightly more votes cast in those cities in 1976 than in 1972. In those portions of Hennepin and Ramsey counties outside the twin cities, population increased by a lower percentage but voter turnout increased by a higher percentage than the rest of the state (see Table 11). How much of this turnout can be attributed to election day registration is difficult to estimate. Although Hennepin and Ramsey counties combined contributed 36.5 percent of the total votes cast in the state, they produced only 30 percent of the election day registrations. Seventy percent of all election day registrations came from outside these counties.

There is no way of determining with certainty whether the candidacy of Walter F. Mondale on the national Democratic ticket had any impact on voter turnout. The sharp increase in voter turnout in the South was widely attributed to the candidacy of a Southerner, Jimmy Carter.

The national turnout pattern suggests that election day registration may have increased Minnesota's voter turnout by as much as 2 to 3

53

Table 12

ELECTION DAY REGISTRATION IN
TWENTY MILWAUKEE WARDS, 1976

District	Ward	Total Vote	Election Day Registrants	Percent of Vote Cast by Election Day Registrants	Percent Democratic Votes for President
4	17	716	323	45.1	68.8
10	1	768	334	43.5	91.6
10	2	816	355	43.5	87.3
6	4	1117	470	42.1	92.9
6	9	843	350	41.5	90.6
7	16	614	245	39.9	77.1
6	3	923	359	38.9	90.0
4	14	281	109	38.8	70.7
7	15	1028	395	38.4	92.6
7	7	866	323	37.3	95.5
15	1	1568	582	37.1	54.8
6	6	1020	374	36.7	96.2
7	8	807	294	36.4	94.7
4	4	832	301	·36.2	91.6
10	13	675	243	36.0	59.4
7	9	978	349	35.7	93.2
16	15	427	152	35.6	58.2
6	11	945	329	34.8	92.4
12	1	604	208	34.4	76.6
4	7	948	323	34.1	45.3

Source: City of Milwaukee Board of Election Commissioners.

percentage points and that it had some impact in the city and rural areas, with slightly more impact in the suburban sections. This pattern, which deviates from the state pattern of voter turnout, indicates that the election day registrants may not have voted the way all preregistered voters voted. If election day registrants had voted as did the others, they would have contributed to an increased Democratic plurality. Because proportionally more election day registrants lived in suburban or rural areas, which are collectively less Democratic, the partisan impact is uncertain.

It is most improbable that election day registration affected the outcome of the presidential election in Minnesota. If one assumes that

President Carter would have lost Minnesota without the votes of election day registrants, then one must also assume that Carter won more than 75 percent of these 454,147 votes in order to obtain the 250,000 vote plurality he ultimately received in the state. There is no evidence to support this possibility.

There is evidence to suggest that election day registration affected the outcome of the state legislative race between David R. Cummiskey and Ron Evans, described in Chapter 2, a race decided by a mere 292 votes.

Wisconsin had fewer than half as many election day registrations as Minnesota. Excluding nonregistration areas of the state, only 10 percent of all votes were cast by persons who registered on election day. Nevertheless, the impact of election day registration is clearer in Wisconsin than in Minnesota. Almost 29 percent of all election day registrations were in the city of Milwaukee, which voted heavily Democratic. The total vote cast for President in the city was up sharply—to 284,896 in 1976 from 260,652 in 1972—even though the city had lost 40,000 population during the four-year period. Twenty Milwaukee precincts with the highest percentage of election day registrants are shown in Table 12. These precincts, with one exception, were heavily Democratic. More than half cast 90 percent or more for Jimmy Carter. The Democratic candidate clearly benefited from the Milwaukee vote.

In the three aldermanic districts in which President Carter achieved his highest percentages, there were 11,900 election day registrations but the total vote increase over 1972 was only 4,200 (see Table 13). This strongly suggests that there were duplications and that many of those who registered on election day would have registered whether or not election day registration had been in effect.

Did election day registration make the difference in the outcome of the presidential election in Wisconsin? The answer cannot be certain but it seems unlikely that the margin of 35,245 by which President Carter carried the state can be attributed solely to the availability of registration at the polls.

The total number of persons who registered on election day was 210,600. Many of these were duplicate registrations by persons whose names were already on the books and who were thus eligible to vote anyway. The number of *new* election day registrations, including those registered from previous addresses, is not known. Based on the voter turnout in nonregistration areas, it appears that voter turnout throughout Wisconsin would probably have been at least about the same level as 1972 had registration at the polls not been available. If so, a *maximum* of about 100,000 votes can be attributed to election day registration. For election day registration to make a difference in the

Table 13

1972 AND 1976 PRESIDENTIAL VOTE AND ELECTION DAY REGISTRATION IN SELECTED MILWAUKEE ALDERMANIC DISTRICTS

Aldermanic District	1972 Vote for President	1976 Vote for President	Vote Increase 1972–76	Election Day Registrants	Carter Votes	Ford Votes	Carter Percent	Carter Plurality
1	12,295	13,675	1,380	3,611	12,308	1,151	90.0	11,157
6	10,457	11,738	1,281	4,024	10,026	1,367	85.4	8,659
7	13,067	14,595	1,528	4,265	11,554	2,654	79.1	8,900
Total	35,819	40,008	4,189	11,900	33,888	5,172	86.8	28,716

Source: 1972 vote for President, *City of Milwaukee Board of Election Commissioners Biennial Report, 1972–73*; 1976 vote for President, candidate votes, Milwaukee County Board of Election Commissioners; Election day registration, Milwaukee City Board of Election Commissioners.

outcome, Jimmy Carter would have had to win no less than 67.5 percent—or more than two out of three—of the votes of all persons who voted *only* because of election day registration. As noted above, Carter did win more than this margin in three aldermanic districts of Milwaukee. In other areas, such as those in Milwaukee County outside the city, and in the growing suburban areas such as Waukesha, President Ford won by substantial margins. Although it is impossible to determine whether the votes of election day registrants differed from others cast in these areas, it would appear unlikely that they did so by the margins required to make the difference. If Carter won 60 percent of the election day registrants who would not have voted otherwise, his plurality of these would have been about 20,000. Without them, he still would have won by 15,000 votes.

Deficiencies of Safeguards against Fraud

Voter Registration Information. The information provided by the voter on the voter registration form in Minnesota and Wisconsin was universally regarded as insufficient to provide identification for post-election verification of questionable registrants. Neither birth date, sex, race, marital status, nor length of time at the current residence is shown on the Minnesota voter registration form. The *day* and *month* of birth are listed as optional information. An investigator seeking to identify a Gale Jones who registered from an apartment address does not know if Gale is male or female, black or white, young or old, married or single, or how long he or she is supposed to have lived at the address indicated.

The Wisconsin voter registration form does list a birth date but it does not provide sex, race, marital status, or length of time at the current address. Without such information or other means of identification, investigators are hard pressed to confirm the identity of such voters, even when they do exist.

At the polls, Wisconsin requires neither proof of identification nor a signature from voters who have preregistered. Election officials enter the voter number in the books, to show the sequence in which the voters voted, but retain no evidence of who actually cast the ballot. If a name has been entered on the lists fraudulently, it can be voted without much fear of detection. The absence of the signature check also means that election officials who wish to pad vote totals may vote as many such names as they desire, without fear of being detected by signatures. Convictions were obtained in Chicago in 1972 when it was proved that multiple ballot applications were signed by the same person. Such evidence would not be available or possible in Wisconsin. Furthermore, because current postelection checks to detect fraud are aimed almost exclusively at election day registrations, the preregistered voters lists are rarely examined for evidence of fraudulent voting.

The Post-Election Check. After the election, the polling place officials submitted the registration cards and lists of voters who had registered on election day to their respective city clerks or auditors for processing. The auditors or clerks were required to verify that each registrant had been properly registered and had voted at the correct ward or precinct polling place. In some local jurisdictions, voter notification forms were sent to election day registrants within a few days of the election, but, in others, at least some of the forms had not yet been sent six months after the election. In the last week of November, attempts were begun to locate election day registrants whose notification form had been returned. In Minneapolis, the voter registration cards were processed and mailed in sequence, beginning with Ward 1 in late November through Ward 9 in May. Table 14 shows the number of voter notification forms by ward that had been returned.

As Table 14 shows, the longer the time between the election and

Table 14
MINNEAPOLIS ELECTION DAY REGISTRATION
POSTAL VERIFICATIONS, 1976

Ward	Mailed	Returned	Percent Returned
1	2,877	80	2.8
2	3,275	293	8.9
3	2,633	254	9.6
4	2,710	171	6.3
5	2,072	287	13.6
6	3,150	570	18.1
7	3,456	575	16.6
8	2,471	435	17.6
9[a]	3,007	419	13.9
	25,651	3,084	12.0

[a]Wards 10 through 13 were still incomplete.
Source: Office of the City Clerk, Minneapolis, May 1977.

the mailing of the notification forms, the higher the proportion of voter notification forms returned as nondeliverable.

The same pattern prevailed in Wisconsin, where the district attorneys received lists of persons whose voter notification forms were returned as nondeliverable. District attorneys without an investigation capability were required to give the cards to local police or sheriffs, who attempted to locate these persons when their own time and workload permitted. Every district attorney's office believed that failure to locate an election day voter at the indicated residence address did not necessarily indicate possible fraud. Again, the greater the time between the election and the investigation, the less likely it was that the person sought would be found. In many cases, the indicated address was a former residence.

In Milwaukee, 2,421 voter notification forms, or 4.0 percent of the 60,415 mailed in November, were returned as nondeliverable by the postal service. They were turned over to the district attorney for further investigation. The district attorney selected about 500 names and addresses in transient areas for further investigation in December 1976 and January 1977. In some cases, the address listed proved to be the former address of the voter who had moved shortly after the election. Follow-up investigations were undertaken in the spring.

To escape detection, a fraudulent voter need only present the minimum identification required by the state or the voucher of a witness. Wisconsin is much more lenient than Minnesota in the type of identification it will accept, but in either state, any person whose application is attested by a witness may vote. A witness may easily satisfy the registrar, and there is no record of what evidence was used to support the witness's identity or residence, nor is there a record kept in Wisconsin of the address of the witness. Two or more months after the election, there is almost no chance of positive identification unless the registrar or another person present in the polling place knows the witness personally and is willing to identify him or her.

This provides an opportunity for a corrupt election official to permit a substantial number of unqualified persons to register and vote without fear of being detected until long after the election. If thirty fraudulent votes are added among 300 bona fide election day registrants, it is unlikely that there will be any suspicion that fraud has occurred.

Vote fraud may escape detection if the voter notification form is not returned by the postal service. Neither Wisconsin nor Minnesota makes any systematic effort to determine whether fraud has occurred if a voter notification form is not returned. No routine check is made to determine, for example, whether the number of votes cast from a single address appears probable, given the size of the building. Even when the voter notification form is returned, there is little likelihood that the matter will be pursued with any degree of thoroughness. Despite charges made in Milwaukee, fewer than one-third of all returned cards were investigated by the district attorney's office. In a transient neighborhood, the lapse of time between the election and an investigation screens anyone wishing to vote fraudulently. And finally, even if it can be shown that a registration address is fraudulent—a vacant lot, or a nonexistent address—the investigating authorities have no clue whatsoever as to who perpetrated the fraud.

Prior to 1976, political parties and candidates were known to have checked voter registration lists and provided election officials with evidence that certain voters no longer lived at the registration address. These voters would then be sent an official notice, and, if they failed to respond appropriately, they would be removed from the list. The names of more than 400 persons at a dormitory address in Oshkosh were reportedly removed after it was shown that the dormitory had not opened the previous September. On another occasion, the names of former students at the University of Wisconsin were challenged before an election and ultimately removed from the rolls.

No official interviewed reported any challenges to the existing lists in Minnesota or Wisconsin before the 1976 general election. A pre-election challenge to a person on the list was generally regarded as futile, because it would not prevent that person from voting from that address on election day.

In brief, the systems employed in Wisconsin and Minnesota are very much "honor systems," in keeping with the longstanding tradition of honest elections in those states. The presumption is clearly that the person who registers is giving his correct name and address and that very little other information is needed from him. The system removes every possible obstacle that registration may impose. At the same time, it is so deficient in procedural safeguards that a fraudulent vote is difficult to detect, and identification of the culprit is next to impossible.

The election day registration procedural deficiencies are compounded by the fact that a voter may register within thirteen days of an election in Wisconsin or within twenty days of an election in Minnesota by "mail." This is sufficient time for the election officials to place the name of the registrant on the polling place list but insufficient time to verify that the address given is correct. The chances are very good that voter notification forms sent to last-minute mail registrants will not be returned to the election office prior to the election. A person who registers fraudulently in advance, as a "registered voter," may vouch for others without additional identification.

In view of the procedural laxity and the failure of the system to provide even the administrative information required to determine election supplies and ballots, some election officials have suggested eliminating voter registration procedures altogether. These officials point out that it is futile to attempt to compile lists of voters, to record changes of address information, and to attempt to keep records when between 10 and 40 percent of the voters at any polling place may appear without prior notice. The North Dakota system of having no permanent voter registration has the advantage of economy, say these officials.

Administrative Problems

Prior to the presidential election of November 1976, the administrative problems of election day registration were relatively smaller and more easily managed. The unexpectedly high turnout of election day registrants, however, did cause major problems in the larger jurisdictions in Minnesota and Wisconsin.

Election officials estimate that it requires an average of about five minutes to process a voter registration correctly at the polls. This allows time for the official to examine the completed registration form for completeness and accuracy, to verify identification and residence, to ascertain that the voter is not already registered from the same address, and to determine that the address is within the precinct and, if necessary, the subdivision. It also provides time to permit the registrar to verify the credentials of witnesses, to administer oaths, and to hear challenges.

In Minnesota and Wisconsin, a thirteen-hour voting day is standard, though there may be deviations in some rural areas of Wisconsin. This allows one registrar sufficient time to register up to 156 persons properly during the voting day, with little time for conversation, lunch, or rest stops. If more registrations must be processed, then the probability of error will increase, and the registrar is less likely to ensure that the form has been completed, that the voter is in the correct precinct, and that the voter or witness has presented proper identification.

There were many precincts in both states which had far more than 156 election day registrants per registrar. Many precinct locations did not have enough space to accommodate separate registration and voting procedures.

Long delays were caused by lack of proof of a current address when a registrant who had recently moved produced a valid driver's license or other identification with the former address. This occurred in transient areas and even more often in college communities, where students may keep a driver's license address for years without changing it. In such cases, the registrar should require a voucher by a witness to verify that the registrant actually lives in the precinct, but with crowds at the polls, this procedure was often omitted. The election contest from Mankato, Minnesota, referred to in Chapter 2, demonstrates that over 200 persons may register in a single precinct without having identification supporting a current residence address.

The long lines in many places caused some voters to be short-tempered and did not encourage registrars to proceed in a deliberate and rational manner. In Wisconsin, many clerks reported that election day registrars and officials said that they would not work under similar conditions in the future. They also reported that these conditions caused some preregistered voters to give up and go home without voting and worked a hardship on the elderly, who waited in long lines. Such comments and observations, widely circulated in newspapers, are quite subjective. It is virtually impossible to ascertain how many people may have been affected by these conditions. On balance, it is difficult to believe that more were discouraged from voting by lines than were encouraged to come to the polls by election day registration. Whether or not the experience adversely affects turnout in future years remains to be seen.

Supplies. In many Milwaukee precincts, the supply of voter registration forms was exhausted. Attempts were made to supplement the original 100 cards sent to each precinct, but not all could be delivered in time to be used. Precinct inspectors were advised to make registration cards by cutting sample ballots into rectangles, 3 by 5 inches, and using the reverse side for registration cards.

One Milwaukee ward registered 582 voters and another 462 persons on election day. The average registration was 180 per ward. Throughout Wisconsin and Minnesota, the pressure of election day registration was greatest in rapidly expanding areas and in college communities, and supplies were rapidly depleted.

In retrospect this situation could have been avoided simply by providing each polling place with additional material. Even though voter turnout increased only marginally on a statewide basis, the variations in election day registration between the precincts were substantial. If registration forms at the polls had equalled 50 percent of pre-election registration, there would have been a margin of safety in virtually every precinct in both states. If paper ballots are used, the number to be provided must be considerably more than 100 percent of the registered voters in order to ensure an adequate supply. This creates a minor problem of ballot accounting and security. If voting machines or voting devices are used, no voter will lose an opportunity to vote for want of a ballot, but there may be a longer wait if the ratio of voters to machines or devices is too great. Both Minnesota and Wisconsin have frequent elections and comparatively short ballots in presidential election years, minimizing the impact of a high ratio of voters to voting equipment. In other jurisdictions, this problem could become more severe.

Interviews with city clerks, district attorneys, and other election officials confirmed the widespread belief that there was much confusion and inadequate control at many polling places. Except in the cities of Milwaukee and Madison and a few other places, a substantial majority of Wisconsin city clerks advocated repealing the election day registration provision. Some Wisconsin communities, including Green Bay, Sheboygan, and West Allis, passed resolutions to that effect. City clerks testified against election day registration before a legislative hearing in early 1977.

City clerks also were in substantial agreement that election day registration renders much of their work throughout the year essentially meaningless. The registration lists for the November election are now most complete and accurate in June of the following year, according to one election official. As an indicator of who may vote where, they are least reliable on election day itself. Many of the city clerks, who have performed a wide range of functions in addition to registration and voting, indicated they would devote less time to registration in future years.

Costs. Election day registration has relatively few simple and direct costs in addition to those incurred in the conduct of personal or mail registration. The largest single cost is the compensation for the election day registrars. This varies greatly by local community both with the number of registrars and with the salary level. This cost may be partially offset by the elimination of other less productive methods of voter registration. Thus far, in Minnesota and Wisconsin, election officials conducted voter registration at least as vigorously, if not more so, than in jurisdictions which do not have election day registration. Other costs incurred by election day registration are the charges related to attempting to identify persons whose voter notification forms have been returned by the postal service, and to the time required to correct deficiencies and errors made in election day registrations. In local communities in Minnesota and in Wisconsin, budgetary factors appear to control what is accomplished. The municipalities spend whatever is available, simply leaving the task incomplete if no funds are available. This was why two large Wisconsin counties made no attempt to verify identification of persons whose voter notification forms were returned. As noted in Chapter 2, Minnesota local communities submitted statements totaling almost $800,000 to the legislature for expenses of election day registration in 1974.

Election Contests. An election contest could result from election day registration if a losing candidate demonstrated either that there was enough vote fraud to reverse the outcome of an election or that, through errors at the polling places, more voters had voted in districts in which they did not reside than the margin between the winning and losing candidates. Either of these contentions would be extremely difficult to document in the brief time between the canvass of the votes and the certification of the winning candidates. The instance of an election reversal described above occurred in a Minnesota city council race where only one vote separated winner and loser.

Through a sampling method, a challenger might be able to demonstrate that a sufficient number of erroneous registrations may have determined an outcome with a larger margin. A court might then permit a further investigation, but there is no assurance of this. Where vote fraud is alleged, specific evidence of probable fraud is usually required before a court will stay the results of an election. There is little opportunity for a losing candidate to document by his own investigation the fact that very many voters voted illegally. The mail verification process occurs long after the winning candidates have been certified and much too late to help the loser's case.

Without the opportunity to identify possibly fraudulent voters in advance of the election and to challenge such voters at the polls, it becomes virtually impossible for a candidate to prove that very many votes have been cast fraudulently. The efforts of the Republican Party and the U.S. Labor Party to obtain recounts in Wisconsin illustrate the problem. Even if a substantial number of voter notification forms of election day registrants are later returned as undeliverable, the election results would have long since been certified. And of course, the mere fact that the postal service has been unable to deliver the form is not conclusive evidence that the registrant did not live at that address on election day.

Although there may be strong penalties for individuals who commit vote fraud, there is very little chance that any election results produced by such fraud are likely to be reversed.

64

5
SUMMARY AND CONCLUSION

Election day registration probably contributed to increased voter turn-out in the presidential election both in Minnesota and in Wisconsin. Each state increased its turnout as a percentage of the voting age population by about 3.5 percentage points, in contrast to an average decrease of 1.1 percentage points nationwide. Of this increase, more than half may have been produced by election day registration. The effect was probably greatest in the city of Milwaukee where election day registration was unusually heavy and where, despite a population decline of about 40,000, the number of votes increased substantially from 1972 to 1976.

Election day registration discouraged voters from registering prior to election day. Election officials noted the absence of the traditional last minute rush before the close of registration prior to the election. The majority of those who did register on election day in Minnesota and Wisconsin were believed to be voters who had previously been registered but had failed to change their address, and some were unnecessary duplicate registrations.

It appears doubtful that election day registration has had much effect on statewide nonpresidential election turnout. In Minnesota, despite the introduction of election day registration in 1973 and the enfranchisement of the eighteen-year-old voters, the total number of votes cast actually declined between the general elections of 1970 and 1974. Election day registration in state primary elections has remained a small fraction of the total vote.

With the exception of the city of Milwaukee, where heavy Democratic registration and turnout distinctly favored the Democratic candidates, there is little to suggest that either party gained disproportionately from election day registration. In Minnesota, suburban and rural areas, which traditionally vote less Democratic than the state as a

65

whole, recorded more election day registration than did the more Democratic areas of the twin cities.

Election day registration certainly did not affect the outcome of the presidential election in Minnesota and probably did not affect the outcome in Wisconsin either.

Election day registration caused administrative problems at the polling places both in Minnesota and in Wisconsin in November 1976. Officials in both states underestimated the number of persons likely to change their address or to register at the polls on election day because there was no way for them to determine how many registered voters had moved away. In many places, ballots, voting machines or devices, and other election supplies were not ordered in sufficient quantities to accommodate the number who actually registered at the polls. In those polling places where estimates were least accurate, long lines, confusion, and procedural breakdowns occurred, and supplies of registration forms and ballots were exhausted. With no other election-related responsibility, one registrar can process accurately and completely about 156 voter registrations in an election day, but many registrars were required to process many more than this. In some areas, especially in Wisconsin, no additional registrars were provided. As a result, identification of registrants and witnesses was inadequate, registration forms were improperly completed, and voters were permitted to vote in the wrong wards and precincts. The error rate in Minneapolis was 47 percent. Many jurisdictions made no attempt to determine how many errors had occurred. Some polling place officials stated that they would not work again under similiar circumstances.

With election day registration, the potential for vote fraud is great and the probability of detection extremely small. Fraudulent registrations may occur if a registrant presents false identification, proper identification of name with a false address, or a false affidavit by a witness. Fraud may also occur if corrupt election officials pass false election day registration affidavits and cast votes in the names of these phantoms. The only two safeguards in Wisconsin and Minnesota are inadequate to detect or prevent these types of violations or to identify the culprits.

The entire burden of ensuring the integrity of the system is placed on a single polling place worker in each precinct. The pressure of time makes it difficult for such officials, many of whom are inexperienced, to insist on proper identification at the polls. Anyone attempting to vote fraudulently—even if stopped by a registrar—loses nothing and may go directly to another polling place. If a fraud is subsequently detected, the registrar is not likely to be able to identify the voter. No registrar can be expected to remember each one of the 100 to 300 election day registrants. Challenges by poll watchers are almost nonexistent in Minnesota and Wisconsin.

The mail verification check fails to identify any voter who has arranged for someone else to accept his fraudulent voter notification form. Thus, the "rooming house" violations prevalent during a more sordid era of national election history are again possible. When a voter notification form is undeliverable in Minnesota, the chances are slim that any attempt will be made to identify the voter. Although Minnesota officials place a challenge notation on the registration form to ensure that the voter will be challenged if he attempts to vote from that address again, this has no effect on any fraudulent registrant or on the election in which the fraud was first perpetrated.

Even in Wisconsin, where unverified names are referred to the district attorney, the election will have been over for a month or longer before the district attorney receives them. With little incentive to spend much time or effort, the local law enforcement officials do not undertake a search immediately, but rather give the time available between more pressing assignments. Failure to find such persons is not deemed evidence of vote fraud. Even if it can be determined that several persons voted from vacant lots or from nonexistent addresses, there is no way to determine who committed the fraud. The identification requested of a voter on the registration form and of a witness on an affidavit is too limited to provide any clues for investigators. Finally, to demonstrate that a fraud occurred, the district attorney must prove that a registrant could not have lived at the indicated address for a few days prior to election day. When an investigation is conducted in a transient area some three to five months after the election, this is most difficult to prove. By May 31, 1977, no district attorney in Wisconsin had reported discovering any evidence of fraud.

With election day registration, votes cast in error or by fraud will be counted equally with valid votes. Discovery of administrative errors or vote fraud occurs too late to prevent votes from being counted, and there is no method of identifying any vote once it is cast. Milwaukee County was still investigating some 500 possible fraudulent votes more than six months after the election. Whether or not any proves to be fraudulent, all have been counted.

Although it has not yet been demonstrated by experience in Minnesota or Wisconsin, it would seem that election day registration is likely to produce more election contests than systems which require that voters be registered in advance of the election. The many administrative errors that permit unqualified voters to vote, or qualified voters to vote in the wrong districts, and the greater opportunity for vote fraud provide a basis for election contests. Evidence of such errors or vote fraud, however, is extremely difficult to obtain during the short period between the election and certification of the winners. Nevertheless, candidates who lose close elections almost certainly will have more election irregularities to support their complaints.

Finally, there appears to be little difference in procedure or concept between election day registration and nonregistration systems. The major differences are that, in nonregistration systems, voters are not always required to provide any identification at the polls and no permanent list of voters is maintained. A signature verification is required in Minnesota election day registration procedures but not in Wisconsin.

Election officials in both states were hard pressed to identify any function for a permanent voter registration system used in combination with election day registration. When election day registration is permitted, the list of registered voters is inadequate to guide election officials in estimating the number of voting machines, equipment, and supplies needed in each precinct, nor does it provide the basic information necessary to prevent vote fraud. Those on the registry need not necessarily vote in the precinct in which they are listed, and persons whose names are not on the list will be permitted to vote. Pre-election scrutiny of voter registration to prevent vote fraud has been almost totally abandoned in Minnesota and Wisconsin.

In conclusion, election day registration probably contributed to a marginal increase in voter turnout, about 1 to 2 percentage points both in Minnesota and in Wisconsin, but it also encouraged many voters to wait until election day to register. It caused confusion and long lines at the polls, and errors were made that permitted hundreds of voters to vote in the wrong precincts or wards.

Although there appears to be little evidence of vote fraud, there has been little investigation to determine whether there was vote fraud. The integrity of the system depends almost entirely on a single registrar at the polling place and the honesty of the voters themselves. There are almost no poll watchers, and the mail verification of election day registrants takes place too long after the election to affect the results or to produce evidence of vote fraud. The forms and procedures offer investigators little information about the identity of possible fraudulent voters.

In states where honest elections are not taken for granted, election day registration would provide an opportunity for vote fraud both for election officials and for multiple voters. The procedures for uncovering election day fraud ensure that the candidates who win by fraudulent votes will be secure against possible contests to their election. Even if fraud were uncovered after the election, the identity and purpose of the culprits would be almost impossible to determine.

If it is widely believed that elections can be stolen, or have been stolen, then the greatest negative effect of election day registration might well be a massive loss of confidence in the integrity of the electoral system, regardless whether fraud actually does occur.

Cover and book design: Pat Taylor